Letters to My People

Inspirational Essays, Poems, and Affirmations

By

Dr. Chris T. Pernell

Copyright ©2013 Dr. Chris T. Pernell.
All Rights Reserved.

Except for the quotation of small passages for criticism or review, no part of this book may be reproduced or transmitted in any form or by any means, electronic or mechanical, including photocopying, recording, scanning, or otherwise by an information storage or retrieval system, without written permission from the publisher.

For more information, contact
Dr. Chris at *chris.t.pernell@gmail.com.*

ISBN-13 978-1490322872
ISBN-10 1490322876
Library of Congress Catalog Number 2013910302

Brand and product names are registered trademarks of their prospective owners.

Printed in the United States of America.

Table of Contents

Foreword..v
Essays...2
   Seeing around Corners...3
   Growing Into and Out of Dreams......................9
   The Culture of Significance;
   the Culture of Success..16
   Righting the Ship..25
   On Changing the World.......................................30
   Occupy Hope..39
   Learning How to Fail
   (Beauty after the Fall)..45
   Finding Patience
   (Waiting on Someday)...51
   Look for Your Mountain..56
   Urban Spring..62
   The Humanist Within:
   Deconstructing They and Other........................68
   Culture as Currency: Building Home Base......73
   The Economy of Favor..81
   Love Matters (The Matter with Things)...........86
   Peculiar People...90
   Exodus: Looking for My Land
   of Milk and Honey..94

Poems...99
   Letters to My People...100
   Not in My Bloodline...102
   Spit and Mud..104
   Hip Hop America...105
   If I Could Put This City on My Back................107
   Go Down, Moshe...109
   Road Map to Greatness......................................111
   Water Will Find a Way..113
   It's Morning...115
   For the Love of Words...117

Reflections and Affirmations...........................119
The Pledge..128

To all people....

Foreword

We have been called to a higher purpose — one greater than our present and brighter than our darkest past. Daily, I cross paths with the broken. I meet souls seemingly void of belief in their promise and expectation for what tomorrow brings. While some need an encouraging word or helpful nudge, others long to hear that they are not alone in this fight. Above all, humanity needs bold and appointed voices to sound out healing and hope. We need change agents who are willing to stand on street corners, behind pulpits, in schoolhouses, the corporate boardroom, trenches, on the athletic field, and all over this land to agitate for progress, challenge us forward, and train up the whole and aspiring. Whether you are confused, curious, on solid earth, ascending, descending, or standing still, we all need someone to speak into our being and pull forth our greatest reflections. Each person is somewhere along the path and process of finding or achieving his or her goals: those who have forgotten their way, those seemingly already there, and the ones just in the middle of the road. Still, while there is breath in our bodies, we have the opportunity to get it right. What is right? *Right* is to understand your purpose. *Right* is to realize your authentic dream. *Right* is your redemption and reconciliation.

We are not born who we hope to be. We are made. Experiences and encounters, trials and failures, successes and victories—they make us. But first we must travel through fires and storms, rainy and dry seasons, harvests of plenty and harvests of few. We must thwart the doubters who seek to vanquish our drive. We must stand against compelling odds. We must labor in love. We must articulate our aspirations and affirm the desires of our hearts. If we listen and understand, we will find our way. But we must hold one another accountable to his or her purpose. Each person must be responsible in his calling. While we are made, we also make. We must bear fruit becoming of our destined greatness rather than that which holds us hostage to our fears and flaws. I truly believe that our greatest moments are yet before us, and, despite our worst moments, which threaten to defame us, we can gut-check and change route. We still have time. Grace abounds. We are made men and women. In whose image we are made is our story to tell.

—Bishop and Dr. Chris

He sent his word and delivered
them from their destructions.

— The Book of Psalms

Essays

Occupy hope. Squat there and refuse to be evicted.
Despite how much you struggle,
hope is a place you can't afford to leave.
—Dr. Chris

Seeing around Corners

Inside that auditorium Cheryl Dorsey's words resounded like a prophet of old. She moved me. A medical doctor with a background in public health, she led Echoing Green, a global fund that invested in social visionaries. She distinguished great entrepreneurs and leaders by their ability to "see around corners." Without question, her words registered. Like a sticky concept that latches on, the thought crystallized in my spirit. There in my seat, I vowed *to see* and imagine forward and then to retreat from that future outpost and build a conspicuous bridge to the present.

To see around corners I had to break through the status quo and advance in meaningful ways—not only to discern and envision the future but also to display courageous faith and stand against the grain. I had to be like Steve Jobs, who innovated a tech landscape that redefined human existence, like any scholar does who challenges our perceptions and norms, or the underdog who disobeys odds and produces an alternate reality. All pioneering firsts must see around corners, create a break in the cycle, and propel you to go where you dare instead of being confined by where you now stand. And so, Dr. Dorsey compelled each person in the audience to be forward-thinking and -seeing and to create progressive, leap-of-faith solutions that made the unimaginable happen.

A year earlier, I ran across a similar idea. In talks with a public-relations exec, she described herself as a thought leader: one who could foretell and conceptualize trends in ways that separated her from the pack. She resonated with me. Then and there, I agreed to capture and formulate my own high-wire ideas, as well as articulate the thoughts of others. Together, she and Dr. Dorsey provided the bookends to a personal epiphany: my high calling was to be a thought leader who could see around corners.

Thought leadership is more than thinking big. It is thinking first. Even greater, it is thinking uniquely in ways that create purpose for others. For me, "thinking big" started from cues in my adolescence, including Ben Carson's *Gifted Hands.* Like the famed doctor, I had to think larger than my block or the urban decay that threatened my city. I had to think bigger than the stereotypes that warred against dreams. Dr. Carson's wisdom felt like home. He conjured up an insatiable sense of duty — thinking big as a birthright. Thinking big was liberating. It was fun. It endowed me with a feeling of substantial worth. Nonetheless, it was not until my adult years that I understood that thinking big meant more than thinking boldly. Rather, it meant thinking ahead of the curve in *nontraditional and imaginative ways.* This, I learned by default after several unplanned events and detours — kind of like the rainbow, which emerges only after the storm, our thoughts should bend light. Our thoughts should inform, challenge, and depict a view of the future. And that's what I heard again that day at the Social Entrepreneurship Summit.

In particular, we in the room fancied ourselves social entrepreneurs, community-minded and people-driven. We built businesses with a social mission. But does it matter what your passion or profession is? In every industry and walk of life you need to be able to see around corners: to rely on insights, creativity, and faith to see through uncertainty in order to accelerate change. Whatever your education or skill level, socioeconomic status or creed, ethnicity or gender, we all are confronted by corners though the type may differ. For anyone, a corner represents where natural sight ends and intuition, imagination, courage, thought-genius, and resolve begin. To put it another way, a corner may appear as an edge, cliff, flat earth, or the unknown, but if problems can ignore such boundaries, then solutions should too.

Leaving the event, I beamed with fresh inspiration, both personal and social. Realizing that a community is only as vibrant as its parts, I needed to share and engage. Since the barriers that corners and hurdles create require diverse and massive attention, I needed to recruit my peers. The more who were available to brainstorm and solve, the greater the outcome would be. Although many are called, still, too few choose. To the contrary, power and the opportunity to develop one's capacity cannot be the domain of the privileged or elite but must be cultivated by both inside and outside forces. Hence, the duality exists: issues of personal agency versus the role of institutions in fair and equitable practices. Even so, I was inclined to see and strike out against corners, the real and abstract, whether physical, spiritual, or emotional. Corners, though formidable, aren't impervious; rather, we must challenge individual, cultural, intellectual, and political biases in order to move forward. Indeed, whole communities will benefit when we find a way to ferry souls from one side to the other, or at least when everyone believes they have a role to play, a swing at bat. I left the summit ready to sound the proverbial alarm! First, yes, to see the corners, and second, to stimulate others to see and believe that these could be overcome — not just to see *if* but to see *how*.

    Back in medical school, I encountered ceilings that looked like corners. Most of them I got around. Others made me question my direction, or the merit of the particular path I had chosen, but never my end. The unexpected has a way of making you cross the street or perhaps turn back. Retreat is a wise strategy when unmitigated danger lies in your immediate sight and self-preservation is the goal. In that case, retreat can serve as a setup for ultimate victory. But when there is still good fight within you, retreat is only premature surrender. The difference, and hence the measure of life, is found in discerning which scenario exists and making decisions accordingly. "Good fight" is not the strength, technique, or even moxie to wage war. Rather, *good fight* is the know-how and wisdom to pick your battles soundly: to LIVE to fight another day and reap your bounty. In every war there is loss, but you must know to which battles you were called. Inspiration and innovation should not be aimless but drenched in purpose. Seeing around corners requires more than serendipity; it needs determined drive. That drive isn't only to "see," as the doctor informed me, but also to "pop" the corner, in the words of a soldier.

The US Marines use a patrol technique called popping corners, where the soldier gets very close to the corner's edge. Not knowing what to expect, the soldier does a weapons check. Then, he pops the corner, thrusting himself forward. Like that soldier, it takes boldness to get within inches of the unknown. It also takes aptitude (i.e., knowing what tools are available and how to use them to overcome the unseen). Still, at any time a soldier can be outgunned, forcing him to rely on so-called intangibles to make the added difference. Not able to see the other side, you must believe that the quality of what you hold will outperform whatever waits. Indeed, you must walk in fortitude. Thinking back, if I had been more daring, I would have maneuvered my battles and corners differently. I believed that success would be more straightforward. But those corners schooled me. They taught me the difference between success and value. *Value* is created when you leverage multiple, diverse talents to achieve a meaningful difference and outcome. When you think from one perspective only, you limit the reach of prospective solutions. You become myopic — good at seeing what is closest to you. Instead, great thinkers and leaders — great individuals — *see* based on various types of resources and insights, and are rightly excellent and brilliant. Daily, I am challenged to walk in this brand of leadership. I am inspired to grow around life's many corners.

Today, I am richer for the courage to see around corners. Innovation, whether social or otherwise, needs awareness, creativity, and the faith to see and comprehend in an environment where others are blinded. While some seem to be gifted in this area, we all could benefit from the practice of imagining and visioning. If we made a priority of such habits, our communities would progress further and faster. While we should be accountable to history and guided by reality, we must be emboldened to build anew. If we would move outside of the silos in which we live and die, and cross into other worlds, our (in)sight would be more diverse and less predictable. Greatness takes a step where others wait. It begs to differ when others conform. It demands that we see around and pop the corner — that we think and build in new dimensions. The spoils go to those who are willing to explore unchartered territory, to dream and forge a way forward when little or nothing is known.

See you on the other side…of the corner.

Growing Into and Out of Dreams

Dreams are a double-edged sword. Either they spark untold happiness or corrode an otherwise fragile soul. But when the latter happens, we misinterpret something crucial to our existence. Dreams are not meant to be landlocked but reinvented—maybe recycled for parts and funneled into new imaginings. Never should a dream hold you hostage. Rather, healthy dreams grow alongside you; moreover, fertile dreams feed from your unique greatness and blossom in the midst of self-discovery. Instead, some build shrines to caged dreams and visit them every so often, as if paying homage could ransom those dreams to life. Even so, a life without dreams is unlived, whereas a lived-in life is the scaffold upon which dreams are realized, replaced, and refined. Thus, finding your authentic self provides the truest inspiration. If dreams are like wings, then your greatest dream will give you the greatest flight.

As a young child, I had quite the precocious dream. Since the sixth grade, I was enamored of the word *neurosurgeon*. Already hooked on being a doctor, I grew enchanted by the idea. It sounded different. It sounded important. It proved a healthy goal, driving me toward excellence. The curious part, however, is that as a young adult, I trusted without question that sixth-grader's logic. I assumed neurosurgery was the only thing I was called to do, not because I possessed a special talent or skill, but because it was familiar to me. Had I been honest, the grown-up me would have confessed that I lacked the technical gift to be a neurosurgeon, even though I had the brains.

Afraid to disappoint my younger self, I stubbornly committed to that sixth-grade ideal. Yet, brain surgery must be more than a romantic notion. Like Dr. Benjamin Carson, you should have gifted hands. Sadly, I didn't. I was born to a family with a peculiar flaw — a benign tremor that showed up unpredictably. Here I was struggling to draw blood but willing myself to become a phenomenal surgeon. Could it be a test of faith, or was it that the dream didn't fit? A lack of faith would make it easier to cope with, because I knew the fix. Not able to bow out, I placed urgent calls to my big-brother pastor, in search of heroic prayers. I needed my hands to cooperate, to wield surgical instruments with both dexterity and grace. Did it matter that I had grown into a different woman, gifted in ways distinct from what that young child imagined? Unfortunately, I was missing out on the fact that I was developing into an excellent clinician. Somehow that truth was smothered by a rigid dream: a dream so inflexible that I tried to convince myself it was achievable, even though I preferred the hospital floor to the operating room.

With practice and grit, I became a solid technical performer. I also was a superb speaker and synthesizer of information and diagnostic solutions.

Growing Into and Out of Dreams

I painstakingly ignored that latter truth—and those who spoke it—because I refused to outgrow my sixth-grade expectations. As a child I perceived excellence to be success at the hardest thing you could imagine. In some ways I was still that person. In medical school I thought primary care was too basic for a big dreamer such as myself. Despite being better at other things, I stayed misguided and naive for as long as it was tolerable. Getting as far as a surgical intern year, I finally realized that I could walk away. Almost giddy, I owned my truth: I did not want to be a neurosurgeon. It was time to stop struggling to perfect a dream that I wasn't called to live. No longer that person, I found health promotion and public health to be wholly riveting and satisfying work. While neurosurgery was an honorable profession, it wasn't mine to occupy. I belonged to a different tribe. Though I had the brain and work ethic for the job, as evidenced by a stellar academic record, it wasn't until I matured that I rightly discerned my space. In my space I could do things others could not. There, I could comprehend my greatness. There, I was empowered to dream authentic dreams fed from a unique vision.

With dignity I put my childhood dream out to pasture. Back to the dust it went, to happen upon the rightful owner, I hoped. I'm not arguing that difficult dreams are impossible or that you should abdicate at the first sign of struggle. Instead, dreams should match the hero within rather than an arbitrary fairytale—no matter how high-minded it is. When the former happens, your struggle has purpose. Without purpose, at best you're wishing upon a fantasy. By definition, fantasies are masquerades that hide you from reality. Rather, a dream is sacred, culled from divine inspiration. It stews from your anointing and takes you before great men. Fantasies, on the other hand, are derived from an active imagination. Fantasies aren't bad, but a dream is profound and, when lived out, able to change the world. Even a dream deferred is richer than a dream unknown, or a fantasy that you only entertain.

Altogether different from fantasies are starter dreams, interim dreams, and mature dreams. Starter dreams are springboards for your ultimate destiny. Use them to explore your potential. If they don't pan out, or you tire of them, move forward. Sometimes, however, we preempt our legacy because we hold ourselves captive to our first dreams, like we do that first love. Either we never get beyond the failure, or we live out our days trying to rescue the past. Rarely do childhood dreams accurately reflect or capture adult appetites. Be patient. Some dreams bridge time and place, as if they're there to serve a finite purpose and challenge us nearer to greatness. Yet, mature dreams oftentimes are found by outgrowing our younger, less-developed selves. Maturity isn't simply a function of age; rather, it's finding your authentic self and understanding your unique difference. I dare you to find your mature dream,

Growing Into and Out of Dreams

because that is where your greatest destiny awaits.

Looking back, I believe my sixth-grade self wasn't telling me what to be but how to be. She was telling me something that took me years to comprehend: greatness is not born out of sheer complexity but out of the unique ability to leave an uncommon mark. Thankfully, I learned the difference. I found the path that remained true to both my aspiration and inspiration: a career as a faith leader and public health physician laboring for social change. In this choice I found an overriding peace, excitement, and the room to explore my true talents. If your "dream" takes you away from your unique gift or some obvious skill, then find the courage to outgrow it and develop a new one. Dreams are not static but stuck people are—stuck in narrow definitions of success. Others are stuck in an untested idea of self.

When I look around, I see people trapped in a guess or a romantic notion about their truer selves. To the contrary, the brave are able to step outside of those boundaries and deliver their difference to the world. Case in point: my brother's dream was to play in the NFL. Football players donned his bedroom wall. Football pads lined the basement, and, absent a little brother, he raised his baby sister on the game. After making his high school team, he was confronted with several realities. He discovered that his four-foot-nine, sixty-nine-pound frame wasn't the right fit, and he didn't enjoy practice. At first, he tried to make up for it by playing harder and riskier. He blocked like someone twice his size, and everyone admired his tenacity and drive. Despite the rush, the lingering hope, and the passion, he walked away after his sophomore year. Fortunately, when football didn't measure up, he planted and invested elsewhere. He continued to dream: as an engineering and economics student, then as a computer scientist and systems manager, and finally as a bishop and theological scholar. His dreams kept growing until he found his highest calling. The lesson is that some remain true to dreams that don't match their capacity or to dreams that they've plainly outgrown. By doing so, we stall our potential and forgo what could have been had we dreamed anew. Had he not faced his heart, he may have sold himself short or imagined little else outside of that boyhood aspiration. I've seen too many wannabe football stars loitering in the present, because the future they once imagined never materialized.

Bottom line: dare to dream until you find your calling. Think of your calling as that niche where you can be whole and excellent. Not to be confused with downsizing, "rightsize" your dreams until you find your uniqueness—not an imposter but the diamond within waiting to be cultivated and harvested. Otherwise, you devalue and miss out on your ultimate worth. Grow your capacity to dream, but be honest. Be thorough and be bold. If you don't, you're left with a stunted soul and a

The Culture of Significance; the Culture of Success

stuck perspective. And that causes you to cling to immature or unoriginal goals. When we're stuck in neutral, we conform to what the larger culture idolizes. We wear the dreams of our family members even if we don't want to, perhaps out of loyalty or expectation. We stingily revere athletic and musical careers when the odds are slim that we can achieve stardom in the arts or sports and regardless of whether we are adequately gifted in that light. We aspire toward the standards: the doctor, the lawyer, or the corporate businessman. But when uninspired people choose generic life paths, they get hobbled results. Instead, wear the dream that is specially made for you—not just any you, but the person groomed by exposure, experience, and enlightenment. Exposure begets experience, and experience begets enlightenment. Exposure begins with diverse opportunities that present constructive possibilities for your future. Experience guides you along life's expeditions and unearths your talent. Experience informs your passion.

Your dream should cause you to be excellent. It should demand greatness. Being great is achieving with purpose beyond selfish ambition. Knowing those stakes, don't guess upon a dream. Do dream, but grow that dream. Grow it by discovery and vision, by strategy and experience. Challenge that dream daily to ensure that you don't miss out on *you* — the next big thing. Your greatest dream is waiting: waiting on you to grow into the person who can possess it. Don't disappoint.

The Culture of Significance; the Culture of Success

Culture is art, identity, and language. Culture is food. Culture is music. It is expectation and appreciation. Culture is comfort and familiarity. To the stranger, however, it may be viewed as peculiar. In essence, culture is that nebulous "thing" upon which human existence and interactions hinge. It can be displayed through faith, fashion, cinema, or dance. It consists of what we learn and commonly practice, as well as what we choose to forget and forbid. So then, there is prejudice in our culture. There is bias. There is insensitivity.

Culture is complex, defined through various norms and customs: How we embrace. How we greet. How we speak. How we mourn. Culture even influences our aspirations as well as our complacencies. Indeed, culture is a powerful medium, at times paradoxical and ironic. Malleable and responsive, it yet stubbornly endures across generations. The features of culture can vary among families, geographies, and political spectra. Usually, we frame the idea of culture as a larger culture versus the subculture, the mainstream versus the counterculture. Which begs the question: How do individuals and communities define what is the dominant culture? How do we choose what to accept or reject? What goes into the rubric that informs these choices, behaviors, and perspectives?

The Culture of Significance; the Culture of Success

Growing up, I was raised in a house where the audacity to be great was expected. It was instilled within us to be trailblazers. So, I viewed being different quite fondly. Though neither of my parents graduated college, my paternal grandfather, Bishop John W. Pernell, DD, was scholarly and degreed with distinction. My maternal grandparents, Reverend Harrison and Inez Gregory, were self-made entrepreneurs. They farmed the earth, briefly owned a convenience store, and Papa served as a local pastor. I carried my legacy proudly. My father, an excellent student and gifted thinker, couldn't afford college. He came up when Jim Crow and racism were ubiquitous. Still, my father was a consummate provider and demanded of us excellence. He insisted that we outperform the norms of our schools and aspire to a higher standard.

Despite having never gone to college, Dad started at the famed Bell Labs cutting grass (the only work that was available), then worked his way into the lab and ultimately became a Member of Technical Staff (MTS), typically reserved for PhDs. After an illustrious career at Bell Lab, my dad went on to teach graduate students at the University of Virginia and work as a research scientist and instrumentation engineer. He never gave us an excuse for being average, because he didn't have one: that sentiment was ingrained in our home life and personal and family identities. My mother was the nurturer. Her love was impeccable. She cultivated in me the joy of writing and public speaking. At our kitchen table, I learned early on the power of the pen and spoken word. Mom primed me for future audiences and gave purpose to my standards. Then I watched her return to the workforce and climb her way up from assistant daycare teacher to the program director for infant and toddler children.

This was our backdrop and all my siblings took pride in being a Pernell. We valued three things: a strong work ethic, education, and faith. In that rich environment, I was reared to be a high achiever. I cherished academic success. Permeating everything was the expectation to be excellent. It sat right next to the music I loved, the dance I lived, and the food I ate. In many ways culture gives you a recipe for life, and in particular mine taught me to appreciate personal and academic success. Hence, I grew up in a middle-income family, where we fought to succeed and build upon our parents' and grandparents' legacies, aspiring higher and bolder, rolling over stereotypes and embarking upon pioneering roles and opportunities. The same culture, which challenged us as individuals, in turn caused us to challenge the world at large. It was but one piece to an intricate social puzzle, though a viable piece indeed.

I understood that culture was more than what soothed me, or gave me definition, more than my color and ethnicity; culture represented those *special ingredients*—that vehicle able to propel me forward and inspire great accomplishments.

The Culture of Significance; the Culture of Success

My culture included standards of faith, art, and academics. That is, I prioritized a culture of excellence, a culture of meaningful success and significance. Growing up in East Orange, New Jersey, at a time when the city was sliding into decay, I clung to those standards. Going to school in Glen Ridge, a nearby affluent town, I clung to my bedrock of ideals. The same foundation in two starkly different worlds kept me rooted in a strong sense of self and consumed with high achievement. Whether at home in East Orange or borrowed away in that privileged suburban town, I remained the same person. Doggedly possessed with the idea that I could be great and that I possessed a (birth)*right* to be successful.

Oftentimes, we hear people agitate for human rights, civil rights, and even individual rights, but too often absent from that public and private fight is an all-out offensive to be great. Too freely, we excuse ourselves from the quest to be great. Sometimes we lack the conviction that our success is needed, when in fact our families and communities need us to be uncommonly successful. Even the world needs it. Perhaps we allow ourselves to be overcome by what appears to be insurmountable odds. Or we take our cues from the pack and the prevailing system (albeit unfair in many ways), and accept average. Sounds silly, but we don't protest and picket *us*. But we should. If our souls were visible, maybe that's what we would see: our inner self persuading and cajoling us to be *more*, in spite of perceived and actual realities. We don't threaten to boycott and strike against mediocrity. But we should. We need to withdraw all stock in low expectations and foreclose on apathy. Think about it. That goes for the privileged and unprivileged alike.

We need to create a personal and community culture whereby we are armed against all forms of assault on our souls, where we reject any idea that is contrary to our self-worth, and demand more on all sides. We must build a value system that prioritizes life success — not just any success but that which adds significance to the human experience. In addition to holding the "system" accountable, we must also hold ourselves accountable. While we need vigorous public debate and civic action, likewise we must not cave in on *us*. We need not settle into insecurities, safe and uninspired dreams, or narrow expectations. Rather, we must cling to bold, life-affirming goals. No one owes us the right to be successful. We owe it to ourselves. What society owes each individual is the *right* to the pursuit of happiness, equal access to opportunities, and the freedom to exercise those rights in a just and open forum. Whether or not we aspire to excellence is a ball firmly in our court. Sure, there are social factors that predispose and hasten certain personal decisions within a skewed or inconsistent playing field, but if we are not the captains of our destiny, then we become pawns instead of empowered actors with autonomy and prerogative.

The Culture of Significance; the Culture of Success

Still, I recognize the overwhelming need for models and pathways to success, and the elimination of unfair barriers. Those who have achieved must reach back and instill and cultivate those seeds of success in another. Together, this fosters a stew of great expectations, shared resources, and innovative solutions that weave a culture where success truly thrives.

As an adult my need for academic success became a mandate for wholesale community progress. I am offended by how many children grow up without the priority to succeed. I am amazed by how many broken adults are trapped and unfulfilled. Our culture in some way acts as an idle bystander as whole communities implode and generations are lost. But when the larger culture fails us, what about our personal beliefs, practices, and norms? What is being done to instigate growth in our most intimate spaces? We are aware of the need for technological advances, then why not the need to grow and cultivate the culture that breeds and feeds our way of life? Why not the need to reflect upon and challenge the backdrop of our living? If we don't grow beyond the legacy of our families and ancestors, then we are not thriving. Perhaps we are simply maintaining or, worse, regressing. The expectation is to go forward and gain ground—to challenge the status quo personally and collectively. Of my friends, I demand a culture of success (herein defined as a culture of significance). Of my family, I demand a culture of success. Of my community, I demand a culture of success. Of my people, I demand a culture of success. I've made it part of wholeness and well-being. I've made it crucial to life. I've made it central to my pledge to be a world-changer.

A world-changer understands the importance of leaving a positive tattoo upon the hearts and minds of the masses. A world-changer refuses to remain stuck. A world-changer has urgency for advancement and progress, not only for those in his or her backyard but also for mankind a world away. A world-changer does not seek the path of least resistance or the road to the quickest victory. Rather, a world-changer values sustainable change and the conditions that enable and promote it. Such a domino effect can begin with the power of one: one committed and creative soul. And that one can set a thousand to flight and that thousand can set a community and world ablaze.

The power of culture to mass-produce salient features and ideas and to engage others in a conducive format is paramount. So why not take advantage of it? Why not have a culture of broad expectations, life success, and self-actualization? It should begin with our youth. It should begin in our homes, and for those without a stable home, it must begin with a mentor, pastor, relative, or credible stakeholder. It begins with those intangibles: the messages that are communicated and reinforced, the goals and actions that are praised and celebrated, and the availability of viable solutions rather than excuses. It begins with parents being accountable and demanding more of themselves before demanding more of their children. It begins with adults holding other adults accountable. It begins with a spiritual and soul awakening. It begins with an enlightened heart and mind. Culture can provoke these things.

Let us commit to mold others to see and nurture abilities. Imagine if each person had that mandate. Imagine if whole communities had that charge. Imagine if institutions felt that obligation. What a universe we would behold! Imagine if our culture was complicit in that idea. Imagine if we built a culture of meaningful significance where success was the journey and not merely the outcome — one where the road to success may be fraught with failures and setbacks, but one in which you *fail forward*. A culture of success is a culture of personal investment and one of vibrant and insightful perspective. I've found that sometimes we fear pushing ahead because of what we may encounter. Or we discredit the effort necessary to produce meaningful results. We use the crutch of inevitability — specifically the inevitability of failure — to dismiss the invitation to be our greater selves. Instead we must step into the unknown knowing that our integrity can override the weight of uncertainty. Out of adversity comes success. Out of poverty comes success. Out of joy comes success. Out of expectation comes success.

And, what is success? Success is the choice to be whole and well, and the act of possessing our unique greatness. It's the expectation that our lives count, not just to us, but also for the greater good. Success is not the fruit of circumstance but the offspring of deliberate intention. Make success your right. Make it your culture, and hold the line.

In a nutshell, a culture of success is a culture of infinite capacity.

Righting the Ship

There I sat in a board meeting for a local nonprofit where the exhausted young leader cried painfully in the face of daunting truths. Together, we faced the sobering reality that our immediate goal was just to "right the ship." Dramatic results would follow if we made that initial course change. In that gut-check moment, we realized we had to right the ship in order to set the stage for future gains.

Fast-forward to a different scenario, where I led a communications project for our ministry. Faced with a lack of capacity and expertise on the team, branding our organization would prove an ambitious project. In a moment of honesty, I had to inform others that they didn't have what it would take to complete the task, though they eagerly volunteered their services. It's not that we needed to outsource the entire project. Rather, we had to right the ship by employing new ideas and talents and assigning team members where they were confident and capable. In the hope of capturing an iconic brand, we needed to turn the page and take a seismic creative leap. I've learned the preliminary goal, oftentimes, is to steer into the path of greatness, even though it may look uneventful and suspiciously plain. As with any change, however, the first step is often the hardest and requires the greatest faith. Diving into the proverbial deep is heroic, but surfacing in the right direction against the current can be strenuous and unglamorous work. Before you can have a sea change, you have to right the ship!

Rightly guiding your boat is an arduous but fulfilling task. It takes courage and fortitude to grab the wheel and turn for dear life. Though my life was above ground, still I had to change direction. If not, my outcome would have taken me away from my highest calling and purpose. For me, it was that drastic. In clinical medicine my health was failing. The cost of success was dimming my star; I had little time or energy to do anything else. My creative passions and ministerial work were at the beck and call of a stingy career that left some of my greatest assets unused. So I had to confront my soul in order to change lanes. But once I did, I found my entrepreneurial drive, community voice, and the road by which to achieve holistic and grassroots change.

I found public health while looking for a management career. Public health and ministry together allowed me to achieve a synergy like none else. Turning into my destiny (and not away) led me down nontraditional paths. And one of those destinations was prison. As a mentor and volunteer at the Essex County Juvenile Detention Center, I grappled with building capacity in the residents and always hoping for a lightbulb moment when those captive hearts would choose a different way. The goal wasn't for these children to hatch into socially responsible citizens overnight. Calvary instead happened more slowly, as we worked together to recognize and define a better way forward—one that could lead these bright minds to safe harbor. The steepest hurdle was the first step in the right direction. For some, it was finding remorse. For others, it was finding peace. Regardless, that change from the status quo was their right-the-ship moment.

Perhaps you aren't a doctor going down the wrong career path or a juvenile offender in some urban jail. Maybe you're a young entrepreneur uncertain of your prospects or a change agent knee-deep in the social landscape and unsatisfied with the pace of change. Regardless, many of us are between concept and outcome. There in middle-earth we find ourselves needing a course correction and battling a strong headwind. We find ourselves face-to-face with the reality that victory happens in stages. Before you pass on your destiny, stop and right the ship. But know that righting the ship is only stage one on the course to future success. Considerable work will still lie ahead.

If you think about it graphically, it's like a setting a bone that has been dislocated. Without realignment you can't begin to heal or regain use of the affected limb. Similarly, in order to have a whole, well life, we must set and align our habits and behaviors according to our desired goals and outcomes. In order to be well or live well, we must *go well*, and that happens one step and one priority at a time. Wellness isn't an end point; it's a lifestyle achieved across time and through effort. We're more likely to "right" costly behaviors by making an about-face, which sets up future success. And that about-face may occur quickly or slowly. Regardless, you have to find a way to halt the slide. To use a medical metaphor, you must stop the bleed first. Only after those corrective actions will you begin to reap gains and genuinely repair the breach, in essence building a platform for forward progress.

So, righting the ship is analogous to laying a good foundation, if not in a literal sense then as a setup to drive future outcomes. Unfortunately, in a results-driven world, little fanfare is made over having the correct foundation. It's assumed that the foundation will be built, but significant interest lies elsewhere—usually at the goal line. The smart builder knows that the end product is only as good as the foundational start. The wise builder knows that sometimes you must rebuild that foundation mid-construction, and pace yourself according to the realities on the ground. At that moment, your greatest push forward comes from redirecting your focus. In other words, righting the ship is regaining control of your destiny despite apparent losses and being able to point your bow in the direction of growth. When we take that sort of ownership over the growth process, we are likely to create enduring change milestones ahead. Imagine the developmental stages that a child travels on the way to maturity and adulthood. Each serves more than a casual purpose, but acts as a rung in an ascending stairway.

Righting the Ship

There comes a time in every journeyman's life when he encounters a cause larger than himself, which demands that he places his ship forcefully and carefully on a new trajectory. When this moment arrives, we have not encountered failure or failed to make a difference. Rather, we acknowledge and experience the truth that change is a stepwise process and that righting the ship is a crucial step. Enlightenment and inspiration can happen in the flash of an epiphany. To the contrary, progress is complex and time-consuming. Progress is forward movement and the substance of real change. But you've got to work at progress. You've got to dirty your hands. All success has a beginning, which starts with righting your ship.

On Changing the World

South Africa changed me: The land and the people. The colors. Their stories. The love and respect they gave. The tears and laughter I shared. The shantytowns and black suburbs, the vast earth and diverse cultures, all changed me. In those two weeks, I matured. Beyond being proud of my heritage, my blackness thickened. My humanity deepened. I valued my uniqueness and cherished my nation. On that visit I learned and lived servant leadership.

It was my third year of medical school when I journeyed to the continent. Traveling across Johannesburg and her surrounding cities, I experienced South Africa's plush beauty. Praying, speaking, singing, dancing, exploring, and just being, I soaked up every dewdrop of inspiration. I went to South Africa on a mission. Knowing there was an anointing to gain, I also knew there was something to give, something owed. Baptized in purpose, I left South Africa profoundly aware of humanity's shared bonds. My visit enriched my mandate to grow communities at home and abroad and to testify of the universal call to change the world and the need to be great. South Africa birthed the song of my spirit: I am a world-changer. Pit stops such as these are markets of growth and valuable exchange. We're demanded to leave behind a testament yet return home with a greater gift to give.

On Changing the World

My brother, Bishop, left the States with a global vision to build, and, being led, he ventured to South Africa. After six months his fellowship with the people of Gauteng province grew into an assembly. So, when I arrived there was an expectation on both sides. Souls flocked to see this peculiar and anointed man's sister. I was eager to serve and not to disappoint. Everywhere, I was reminded of a purpose larger than self. Humbled by other's expectations, I committed in my heart to be more excellent. Indeed, there is a sizable difference between perfection and excellence. Few find perfection in any given field, but all are capable of excellence, whether in their love, thoughts, or deeds. In essence there should be a standard in your living—a standard in your love, service, expertise, and gifts. Bishop gave me the freedom to experience all that Gauteng had to offer as he departed for Cape Town with a band of brothers. Alone, I felt safe knowing that I too had been led. I trusted in the opportunity. My soul was ministered unto by the many who had something to tell. So I listened intently. In return I spoke at church services, homes, and open-air gatherings. We traded conversations, hopes, and dreams. My mind eagerly recorded every moment. I had to be able to translate with accuracy and urgency the wellspring of joy and vitality I encountered.

My American accent stood out. Upon speaking with me, folks repeatedly shared how America was the land of opportunity and dared me to confront any stereotypes that I held about Africans. It gave me conviction to ensure that my beloved America lived up to her reputation. I returned home, and to Durham, North Carolina, where I evangelized on the streets, telling all that we had a responsibility not to sell out the hope that existed across the globe. Rather, we had to squeeze every ounce of prospect, no matter how difficult or contested, out of our nation. To be faithful to the seeds of greatness within us, we needed to challenge our environments, beat back adversity, and be more excellent. These are the sentiments that the people of South Africa dared within me. I could not speak about global change; I needed to live that change. I owed it to the eyes, hearts, hands, and souls around my neighborhood and the world.

So I made it an objective to train up world-changers, even out of those who had never left their home turfs. Changing the world is a mind-set if not a place. We as humans need to be global in perspective and local in reach. If we start locally, ultimately we can reach outside of our networks to affect lives worlds apart. Doing so will make the world a smaller place, but make those who live within it larger in thought and deed. The relationships I established in South Africa have stayed with me, to varying degrees. In essence South Africa hasn't stopped changing me, and I hope neither have I, it. We've stayed connected through cyberspace and shared opportunities. Thought-partners there have visited me here, and our dialogue and connection have grown. Our exchange continues to flourish around the idea that all humans can aspire to be those change-makers who operate in abridged cultural space to articulate common struggles and hopes and *best-principle* solutions. Thanks to South Africa, I've parlayed what happened in those two weeks to a decade's worth of work here on the ground.

If South Africa challenged me to bring change on a global scale, then opportunities at home schooled me in the power to change myself and others. We owe it to one another to change the spaces wherein we live and die. Our existence would be fuller and our legacies richer if we did. Often I think back to my grammar school days. I reflect on that predominantly black urban school where I learned an appreciation of self. Elmwood encouraged me in the belief that I could be excellent. The very idea consumed me. But what good is your excellence if it is not used to shape the world about you? I had to learn to transform my expectation of self and others into a spark plug that ignited my peers to equivalent levels of success.

Back then I was preoccupied with a different flight. Not unlike the white flight out of Newark some decades earlier, I represented academic flight. My educational pursuits took me away from home, literally and culturally. In search of equal opportunity and the chance to be academically competitive on a national scale, I went to school out of district, which I found palatable as long as I stayed true to the understanding and ideals that represented *home*. High school was a crash course in many of life's major lessons: how to swim upstream, rise to the top, and still be a difference-maker. Those high school years were critical, because they taught me tenacity and never to settle into adversity or accept the status quo.

As a tuition-student at a nearby suburban high school, I commuted between East Orange and Glen Ridge daily. In and out, I ferried between two worlds not wholly dissimilar but separate enough that I felt the difference. For the most part, my high school was culturally homogenous. Despite being one of the few black or minority students, I found a way past the isolation and made the environment more tolerable. If I could affect hearts here, I told myself, I could handle whatever came after here. Glen Ridge became my social adventure, and I learned to thrive. On the hunt for a better education, still, I had to use my voice to color in the pages of my experience.

Though it involved sacrifice, my choice to attend Glen Ridge was right, and the schooling was more than academic. Alongside being excellent in the classroom, I labored to impact the school's culture. Filling the void partly meant forming a step team and the Black Awareness Club, and, more importantly, advocating for a more inclusive literary curriculum. In particular, the Black Awareness Club took a field trip to see the movie *Malcolm X*.

On Changing the World

Afterwards, I put up a display about Malcolm in the school library. Whenever an oral project or book report lent itself to my cause, I broached unfamiliar and uncomfortable topics with a scholarly appeal. From Malcolm to the Black Panther Party to black literary masterpieces and the historical hypothesis that black explorers came to the Americas before Columbus, my classrooms became think tanks for bold thought. My peers and teachers for the most part were engaged, and together, we all were changing—each at his or her own pace. In my growing mind, I wanted to "liberate" them—if not from ignorance then from fears and assumptions. Standing out in that environment liberated me. Seeking to improve my academic experience and enlarge the perspectives of my classmates was an empowering lesson in organizational change.

My classroom pursuits enlightened me in diverse ways and prepared me for the life I would lead after Glen Ridge. An important lesson I learned is that although change can be uncomfortable, it awakens you to a truth that otherwise would have been ignored. And so it felt exhilarating and purposeful to introduce variety into a somewhat bland and stifling atmosphere. Here I was getting a top-rate education while giving one. I didn't fully grasp it then, but this is what it means to be a change-agent. I didn't solve America's race problem, nor did I fix what was broken in that small town, but after four years I made an impact on my development and I hope that of others. Long before

South Africa, I learned the power of change. As an adult, however, I gained a greater understanding of the call to bring change—inwardly and outwardly, abroad and near. In life, learning is a twofold pursuit. There are things that the subject and the professor alone are meant to teach you, and there are things that you are meant to discover about yourself, which inform how you give back and teach others. A world-changer sees learning as a growth industry and the world as a universal canvas of discovery. In order to bring enduring change, you must recognize that every situation has potential meaning. It's your perspective and outlook that drives that meaning for the good or the bad.

I believe it's that drive compelling me forward: The call to be different. The call to bring change. The call to be changed. Such a mandate should not be viewed selfishly. Rather, it must be an organic process. Change comes first to the person—often by direct experience and other times through enlightenment—then to like-minded or receptive others, and finally to the masses, if deemed valuable, through systems, solutions, and brave thought. Looking about the sea of humanity, I am amazed at the collective potential to institute change; but we are in many ways socially and politically wired to fight against it, which can be costly. But everything has an associated opportunity cost (i.e., what you give up in order to acquire something else). To love more, the cost is your hate, indifference, or your love for another thing. Change is built on

On Changing the World

choice. Outside of repressive political regimes or developmental disorders where choice isn't realized, in order to bring change or to perpetuate change a person must choose to participate fully. By practice, we humans should evolve and grow to be our better selves. As a direct result, our growth should cause positive change as it relates to our environments, cultures, and societal well-being. If we each purpose to be vessels for constructive change, then not only would we be greater than our former selves, but also our societies would reap the benefit. And yes, not all change is created equal. Rather, the merits of change, whether it is meaningful or not, will be attested to by what is produced. I say, taste the fruit, and see if it is good.

The moral of the story: find a place — whether literal or abstract — where you are different in some meaningful and noticeable way, and sojourn there not only to learn about yourself but also to learn from others, and then employ that knowledge to change your world and others'. To be a difference-maker, you must first understand the power of being different and own it. Once you do so, you allow yourself to create a vivid and dynamic difference for someone else and to transform their understanding the same way yours was changed. Too often, being radical is confined to an unacceptable box. Rather, be radical by leaving the safety of what you know, and travel — physically, culturally, in a book, through conversation, or spiritually — and be enlightened in a way that being stationary or stuck in the familiar never would have afforded. Then, and only then, can you dare to change the world. The world won't be changed by conformists or isolated revolutionaries. The world will be changed by the living, who breathe in the same space as others and impart a wisdom otherwise not imagined and create a fruit, though peculiar, strangely necessary to personal and collective growth.

What if we each aspired to leave a mark upon mankind in some valuable manner and that started within and then spread like a contagion without to our homes, friends, communities, and across borders and through cyberspace to distant worlds? What if the profound change was actually something simple? We could change the world by loving more, respecting more, sharing more, forgiving more, imagining more, challenging more, building more, learning more, helping more, knowing more, and being more.

Occupy Hope

Occupy hope. Squat there and refuse to be evicted. Despite how much you struggle, hope is a place you can't afford to leave. With hope you're fitted to overcome the darkest of hours and envision your way through unsafe and uncertain passages. Without hope you dry-rot or reach a stalemate. Worse, you become a hostage of your environment or your genetic legacy. But life is worth more than what has been passed down, left over, or denied; life is lived in the affirmative, and hope is its engine. It gives you the ability to create. Indeed, I've known the sting of disappointment many times over, yet the letdowns pale in comparison to the horizons after each storm. The rainbow is a covenant sealed in hope. Despite the chance for redemption, disappointment weighs heavy on the soul and brings you into inescapable conflict, whereby you find yourself stuck in the why and what-ifs. Inwardly, we rationalize that this could not have been the intended outcome. Still, the soil after failure is far richer and riper for change.

It's important that others understand that my success is not magic and that I've failed. I've failed privately and publicly. I've failed small and large. I've failed multiple times at the same thing. And I will fail in the future. Regardless of my failures, a new dawn always emerges and hope springs eternal, which has fueled my success. Smart work (not just hard work), the insatiable drive to be excellent, and my belief in a greater purpose all supply my hope. A life without hope is a jail sentence. Yet some are willingly committing themselves to prison.

Of course, you're better off risking failure than hiding from opportunity or believing that opportunity doesn't exist. Going through disappointment is healthy but the lack of hope is not. Disappointment is a reluctant teacher. You learn character. It instructs you in the art of resiliency and innovation. It informs how and who you trust and your priorities. But if you've lived through more than a few encounters, you've come to understand that disappointment is part of the life-cycle of success. Disappointment should stir you to reach outside your present situation and to imagine a different future. Though disappointment plays the role of antagonist, hope, if heroic, can win out. It's all in your perspective. Otherwise, you risk growing discouraged. Discouragement is expensive, because it gives you permission to sell yourself short and to be the lesser, because someone or something hasn't recognized or sanctioned your greatness. Instead, hope is like a garden. You must cultivate it. Nurture and water it. Feed it with sunlight. Encourage it with like-minded souls. Prepare it for that dry season. Prune it if need be, and know when to uproot and plant elsewhere. Hope is the seed that becomes your fruit. It matters what you do with that seed. Yes, hope matters. It is the beginning of belief and places success within reach.

Occupy Hope

I am reminded of two parables: one about the sower and the other of the talent. In the parable about the sower, we're taught that the soil where you grow your garden is critical. I raise this illustration to prove that too often we accept the lot that we've been given instead of searching out new land. Sometimes a change of scenery, whether emotional, mental, or literal, can change your inspiration, aspiration, and understanding. There is enough space on this earth to imagine and define your plot without being denied equal access, being limited in outlook, or preying upon another person's share. Although society's presentation of choice can be disingenuous or skewed, you still owe it to yourself not to surrender or accept the status quo. Life is not fair, but hope is an equal-opportunity gig. And though opportunities are not always equitable or just, hope demands that you understand your worth and fight to realize a way out, through, in spite of, and by all means necessary. Make the investment in you that will change your destiny.

In the second parable, the king disperses talents to his servants. For the most part, the servants invest their talents and have an increase; however, one servant buries his talent and returns that same share to the king upon his arrival. Being limited in his thinking and operating off fear instead of faith, the servant does not gain anything in the end. When you fail to invest in or grow your potential, you rob yourself of years' worth of returns. The crime is not just in the present but also in altering your future state. When you stay in the expected or rationalize your actions based out of fear or from a position of lack, you fail to secure a greater outcome. A builder's perspective is to build up from a foundation. Likewise, if you're not hoping and believing up from the legacy of others, including your family, then you lack vision. Too often, I hear children tell me they will achieve what their parents or families achieved. That's not enough. Because then your life has been determined by others even before your first breath. Rather, each successive generation should aspire to achieve greater (if not in number then in impact) and smarter. If not, your hope is common by your own standards, and average hope produces an average outcome. The greatest success, and not necessarily the richest success, is success that is original yet cumulative and that builds creatively and distinctly from a previous foundation. That is the power of authentic hope. Do you have it?

The difference between hoping and wishing is significant. Hope is a springboard for action and carries you in the direction of your desired outcome, whereas wishing designates you to imaginary space. To the contrary, hope is empowering, and should move you forward. You know when you're wishing, because you don't take identifiable steps toward the hoped goal. Rather, hope pulls at you and drags you nearer to the finish line. Still, it is not the culmination of a thing, but a catalyst. Hope without strategy, however, is barely hope, and a

Occupy Hope

setup for burnout. Hope is sustained by progress, whether concrete or emotional. Furthermore, hope with strategy becomes true vision. It is my hope that you're not wishing but hoping, and that in hoping you're doing, and in doing you're progressing and moving forward, and in progressing you're achieving and realizing smaller goals on the path to a larger success. Hope starts you off with training wheels, but then your hope grows, and your faith right along with it. Next, you're hoping while riding a different bike—without training wheels. You get it. Hope is transitional. It's the linking verb that gives the sentence proper meaning and allows you to communicate clearly and compellingly.

Be full of hope. Fall down. Experience a failure, but don't become one. When you fall, fall forward. Fail forward. Just don't stop. Even when you're disappointed, don't resign yourself to failure or choose a lesser option. Rather, get back up and hope again. Remember, hope is critical to your success. Otherwise, when you stop hoping, you get stuck in your failures. Without hope, failure becomes like quicksand. With hope, failure becomes enlightenment. Rather, if you stop hoping, you stop believing, which short-circuits your potential. And when you don't believe, you refuse to make any genuine effort, because you think it's futile. Get it. The lack of hope is a trap and downward spiral. The greatest risk is not a bold initiative. Instead, the greatest risk is a life lived without hope or with too little hope. That life is uninspiring and leads to inaction and becomes a wasteland for fear, bitterness, regret, discouragement, and apathy. Imagine you're at center court, and the referee calls jump ball. With hope you anticipate the win. You jump a little higher than the opponent and set yourself up to have the final possession. Occupy hope, and you'll occupy a greater dream and ultimately have a greater outcome.

Learning How to Fail (Beauty after the Fall)

Perfection is not merely science fiction. In many ways, it is unique to each person's perspective and not a single absolute. When perfection is rigidly defined as the absence of error, too few can find it. Instead, perfection is excellence at work. Only, it begins in excellence and ends in greatness. *To be* perfected is to be that fitted puzzle, your potential realized – the whole and not the part. My motto: make perfection out of your mistakes. In other words, don't concern yourself with being faultless. Rather, be preoccupied with finding your greatest purpose and obeying it.

In Scripture we learn perfection's truer meaning: faithfulness to what you were called to do and playing your ordained role. We know this because of the three wills: the good, the acceptable, and the perfect. We're taught that there is a good will for your life (basically, any good thing), an acceptable will (what is permissible), and a perfect will (where you achieve the fullness of greatness and life success through steadfast adherence, and not necessarily where you encounter little or no resistance). This understanding is different from being without fault or sin or being incapable of wrong. It is more humane and actually feasible. To be perfect is to be whole, complete, and mature. To be perfect is to be obedient to your calling. Even the perfect stumble. Even the perfect fail. Moreover, what if we understood perfection to mean the beauty that comes after the fall? Mankind is fallible. Yet, despite humanity's flaws we can find purpose and inspiration through failure. Again, we can find the perfect. We can find that afterglow.

There is no successful person who hasn't experienced failure, and, in particular, who hasn't experienced public failure or failure on a large scale. If you seek success, then you must know how to fail responsibly and get back up. I once heard my bishop say that you have to learn to fail forward. Imagine tripping across the finish line. Imagine falling flat on your face. Imagine not measuring up but knowing more than you knew before you started. These are all examples of failing forward. I've learned that vital lesson. In life, with every opportunity comes the chance to win or the chance to fail. It's not as basic as saying there are winners and losers. Instead, how you win or how you fail will determine if history records your performance as a victory or a loss. Indeed, I've known many successes, and I pride myself in excellence, but I've failed too. I didn't match at my preferred residency. I lost a political election. I was denied entrance to academic programs. My performance was less than stellar on standardized exams. Still, each time I was faced with the choice to be more excellent and find a more excellent way forward—to find perfect. Through each failure you learn something important about yourself. You may learn that losing was the better blessing. If your worth can be found only in winning, then losing will kill you! When

Learning How to Fail (Beauty after the Fall)

you determine your worth by your promise, then you're constantly living out your capacity and vying to convert potential energy into kinetic energy.

Recently, I was at Shabbat service where a bright, young rapper delivered his crowd favorite, "Failure." In the song he raps about rising from failure to prosperity and fame. He raps about giving "failures everywhere a choice." Short but loaded, that lyric struck a mighty chord. Too many people who fail don't believe they have the choice to get up and succeed. Too many souls are trapped in the past, stuck on Pause instead of hitting Play and living a distinctly different tune. When you fail you can choose to picture that fall as a momentary setback and not a reversal of fortune or your doom. The greats tend to recover quicker and use failure as a canvas for reinvention. The pain of failure tries to convince you that the letdown is a hurdle too high to overcome, but the richness of failure invites you to push toward victory from those less than desirable circumstances. Remember, odds don't have to work against you. Odds can create the perfect storm from which brews unexpected greatness and peculiar beauty. This is a truth that must be engrained in our culture, especially for the most vulnerable among us. Otherwise, we are destined to perpetuate failure rather than breaking that troublesome chain.

It is easier to learn from failure if you don't believe it is intrinsic to whom you are. See failure as a mere fact and not as an absolute. It isn't the only fact but a blip on a timeline—one point in a collection of events—that, alongside your victories, speaks your ultimate truth. People go wrong when they believe they are failures because they have failed. There is a powerful difference. If failing made us failures, then multitudes would have been counted out of the race, never to be heard from again. You can't allow failure to silence you, because if you give it permission, it will smother you into surrender. Rather, you should have a not-on-my-watch mentality! If not, failure will bully you into acceptance.

With each day comes the promise of a new canvass. As a life artist, we hold the ability to innovate beyond yesterday's headlines. Our power lies in going forward from peak to peak, through valleys, trenches, and dark tunnels. If you believe that your best is ahead of you, then you always have something to reach for beyond the darkness of the moment. Those who feel counted out act accordingly and sabotage their ultimate success. It's hard to comprehend the horror of a suicide bomber. Yet, when we undervalue ourselves and undermine our future success, we inflict brutal self-damage, sometimes fatal, and lessen or alter the impact we would have had on others. We change our destiny and outcome. We give failure power it never should have. Take back your destiny and dictate to your failures the whole of your story. It is within your right to police failure, confine and restrict it to the tiniest of space, giving it little or

Learning How to Fail (Beauty after the Fall)

no air to breathe. It is within your right and best interest to forget failure until it is no longer raw, and then to mine it like the earth for hidden gems and pieces of coal capable of becoming diamonds. Some failures are highly toxic. That's when you fail backward. Others lull you into complacency. That's when you fail and lose no ground. Then there are those failures that are ripe and rich with potential for transformation. In this last case, those skeletons provide the fuel and framework for building your way forward — building your masterpiece.

As a young performer, I was trained to learn from my mistakes. Otherwise, you will be primed to repeat them. After learning, however, you've got to keep moving and not linger in regret. Even my grammar school chorus teacher forced us to put one note in front of the other. A righteous melody can be made from the shortcomings of our past encounters. There is a symphony waiting on you for bright notes and dark notes, high notes and low notes. It is the right mixture of sounds, which produces harmony. Apart from the whole, your blend may sound odd, but altogether the acoustic experience is rich. So, don't *sing* your failures out of proportion to your successes. Keep them in the proper perspective and context. Don't let them get too rowdy and quiet your hope or convince you that you are beholden to them. Get the upper hand. Walk as the captain of your legacy. It may sound counterintuitive, but in life you will fail at something. Still, expect to win. Knowing that the life cycle of success involves failure, still expect to win. Each time you step up to bat, aim for the fences. If you hit a foul ball and strike out, get another at bat. If you clear the wall, then clear the bases. If you hit a pop-up that is caught, make a daring try for first base. If not, get back in the lineup. If you hit a line drive, bring as many runners home as possible. If you find yourself in a slump, keep swinging. It's your only way out. As long as you're swinging, you can improve your batting average.

Remember, failure is a setup for a comeback, and the greater the comeback, the greater the glory. But in order to obtain the glory, you've go to go through something: perhaps some death, some setback, or some fall. It's up to you to create the beauty after the fall. Then, you've learned how to fail, and in doing so you've learned how to live the greatest success. And, you've found your perfection.

Finding Patience (Waiting on Someday)

And not only so, but we glory in tribulations also knowing that tribulation worketh patience and patience, experience and experience, hope.
— *The Book of Romans*

Finding patience is brave and consuming work, but reaping the spoils of patience is sublime. It's not like patience can be borrowed. It's manufactured only within the native host. You've got to labor for it, but when it delivers, you're sure to feel empowered. Patience doesn't hatch overnight. It's groomed through struggle and indeed delay. Yes, delay. How else do you know you're patient other than to endure the wait and long-suffering? The secret to waiting is to live in the direction of your goal, ever increasing in expectation. Then the wait perfects you. Otherwise your patience is an impostor for bitterness and despair. Often when I speak with young children, I'm asked how did I complete so many years of schooling. I guess that to a child, it seems as if I've spent my entire life inside a classroom. However, I view it quite differently. You will be patient and sacrifice for what you believe is your highest calling — your unique life-print.

Have you ever waited on someday? A funny thing about waiting: how you wait is as important as why you wait. If your wait is a standstill, then *someday* will never come, because you won't have made the proper investments or steps toward achieving your goal. I've waited on many promises; yet, my wait wasn't idle but full of action—planning and pushing myself toward the intended target. Sometimes I found that someday was not a specific outcome; rather, it was the process of finding meaning in the journey or discovering an alternative end result. *Someday* may seem like that mythic culmination of all you've waited for, but someday can be less dramatic. Actually, someday is each day we choose to live and inhabit the moment with purpose and aspiration. When you wait in this manner, you keep yourself ready and available for the right timing. When we're impatient, we rush success or miss it altogether, because it comes in unfamiliar circumstances and conditions, somewhat off-schedule, or it doesn't hold true to what we like or expect.

Rather, judge *someday* as the moment that offers the greatest opportunity for growth and the chance to walk in your highest calling. Even if you hit the obvious mark, endure until the time presents itself to walk in your greatest impact or legacy. That's when your hope will have borne out the greatest success. What sustains such a wait is the integrity and nobility of your hope. Find hope, and you will find patience. What is dangerous about the wait process is if after the wait, you still believe you're not good enough or you're undeserving of success. Imagine waiting only to delay the inevitability of failure. Why bother? Then you're not waiting. Rather, you're choosing to fail on a payment

Finding Patience (Waiting on Someday)

plan instead of risking and striving for greatness.

Of all the things I've waited for in life, the wait to find my true self has been the most rewarding. When I thought my greatest gift was to be an excellent doctor, I heard the inner cry to be more excellent and to somehow combine public and community service with public health. Defining that lane has required personal creativity, an innovative spirit, and the dexterity to traverse two worlds, which at times are at odds with one another: one rooted in passion and the other in dispassionate expertise. Still, where they meet and borrow from each other has been a delightful mix. Throughout my personal and professional journeys, what has resounded is the guiding belief that patience happens when you find your charisma. When you leverage your specialness and use it as an asset to live purposefully, you become charismatic, and charisma informs and feeds your hope, which cultivates your patience. The more charismatic I've become, the more hopeful I've been in my ability to make a meaningful difference and hence, the more patient and resilient in living up to the promise. Too many of us don't live through the wait. Rather, we wait and hold our breath. It's not patience if your living is compromised. Instead it's torture, and no good thing can come of torture. Torture is inhumane.

Patience is the gift to wait and live with the expectation that each day holds a unique promise if not the desired end. Patience is found in the midst of laughter and even tears. Patience is like growing pains. On the other side of the discomfort or tension is maturity, and with that maturity comes new benefits and challenges. Patience is not always easy but does reward according to its merit. The better and more excellently you wait, the richer your bounty is. Imagine that patience pays a dividend that depends as much on what you gain while waiting as whether you achieve your stated goal. There have been times when I was patient and waited on a particular day that would never materialize. Still, I reaped amazing benefits, because I was perfected in my trial and came away with a perspective that enabled an alternate and no less fulfilling outcome. Growth during patience means you may no longer fit your original want; however, you grow into a new desire that could have been discovered only through your trial. Frankly, this is the hindsight that patience affords, and the wisdom that spills into your next wait.

When you lose patience, you develop a cheating heart and betray the great thing you were called to do. When someday takes too long (because we fail to realize that each day is pregnant with opportunity and not some magic day), we feel compelled to react, often prematurely. When you dismiss the experience of the wait and the likely discoveries therein, you cheat on your destiny. Rather, during the wait period, I found something more than patience. I found the courage to be long-suffering. You become long-suffering when

Finding Patience (Waiting on Someday)

you become a champion against odds, injustices, and public failures and likewise possessed with the idea that you can overcome time and achieve great things. And that has been the secret to my life success: the ability to fail forward and still have a greater expectation than I did the day before. In life I've learned that every day lived is a day closer to attainment. So, in fact, the wait is filled with micro-successes: stories of climbing small hills in the run-up to scaling that tall mountain. Those small feats become the anchors that buoy your hope and pace you forward to endure your particular race, whether it's a sprint or a marathon.

Look for Your Mountain

I'm coming up on the rough side of the mountain.
I'm doing my best to make it in.
— Bishop F. C. Barnes

Ask any great warrior, and she will tell you that the way to victory is *through* — whether a tempestuous storm, iconic battle, or inconvenient trial you must contend in order to get to the other side. Truly, we all want to get to the place called *there*. There is the proverbial greener grass, the sugar and spice, and the stuff of dreams. And, quite frankly, we prefer the less arduous route. Yet, each of us has a story we must tell and a journey our shoes must walk. We want the heaven, but it seems as if we've been asked first to endure the hell. Don't be mistaken: no one is exempt from struggle. The measure of struggle is different and particular to your situation. Still, in some measurable way, there is a mountain with your name on it, calling you out like David did Goliath. Only this time, you are the shepherd David, and in your hand is a stone, and against the mountain it seems feeble, but you know, deeply buried within your heart, it's enough to win.

As sung in Reverend F. C. Barnes's iconic gospel anthem "Rough Side of the Mountain," many heroic and daunting fights demand more grit than brute strength, more heart than muscle. Indeed, victory road is strewn with hurdles and setbacks, perhaps even defeat. Though defeat

Look for Your Mountain

may appear as a red light, it doesn't have to stop you. Rather, the veteran sees defeat as a caution that causes her to reevaluate the way forward. In life mountains are inescapable. They litter the path to the greater you. They are majestic from afar, but up close the jagged rock can be frightful.

Still, the mountain teaches you to find beauty in adversity. Even though you may trip and fall upon the rock, for those who seek it, there is beauty after the fall. There is a peak to match the valley. When confronted by those brave souls who have climbed such literal wonders, I am reminded of man's ability to prevail. Even mortals can defy natural laws. Mountains, however, demand of you an uncommon faith and fight. You must outdo your best if you are to face any mountain and win. Yet this is where we encounter the most difficult part of warfare.

Frankly, many among us stumble over the notion of doing more than our best, because we conceive of it as a rigid absolute and not a moving target. When we hit that ceiling, we begin to accept failure, because we say there is nothing better within us or that we've done all that we are capable of doing. Yet any champion or elite athlete knows that your best must be challenged. Otherwise, some opponent will come along and call your best average. Likewise, the mountain requires you to be better than your best. And how well you respond to this test determines your lot among the good, the better, or the great.

Too often, however, our expectations of self and one another fall desperately below the merits of the human spirit. We handicap ourselves and choose the appearance of calm over the substance of a hard-fought battle won. Self-preservation though instinct can be a drawback when we are afraid to enter the arena because of what we may lose in return. In the wake of Everest, we cannot afford to crumble. Regardless, if you choose to run from your mountain, it will find you. So, be a *king*. Look for your mountain, and find your way to the top. And after you have arrived at the summit, after the bruises and scars on the way up, reach back and pull up another soul. There is always room at the top, but only for those who dare to climb. There is a mountain with your name on it, and the summit belongs to the brave.

If we trace back the steps of greats who stood for causes larger than themselves, we will see that every movement and meaningful fight started with a mountain. But assuming the summit doesn't always signal instant victory. Sometimes the mountaintop is a vista from which to survey the fullness of the land and see the manner of battles that lie ahead. It takes mental fortitude to peer out across the future and see trouble on the horizon yet remain in the fight. And so, I reflect upon the legacy that great warriors have left us. Some of these heroes are counted among the fallen or the slain, but they withstood until successors were named

Look for Your Mountain

and the battle was safely in the hands of those who were willing to take the mountain and the land on the other side. For every Moshe there is a Joshua generation, but we must betray timidity and follow the blueprint to greatness. Indeed, we've been made joint-heirs to a certain destiny by more than pedigree and circumstance but calling and purpose.

Mankind has lived through all manner of brutalities—human and environmental, civil and political. Somehow the human race has always gotten beyond finality. No mountain has stopped us yet. So why should you be any different? If you think about it, history teaches us that man has found a way to survive horrific feats. Moreover, the fact that you are standing testifies of someone in your lineage overcoming what looked like insurmountable odds. Despite genocide, holocaust, Middle Passage, famine, epidemic and war, you are alive because you hail from survivors. Someone in your lineage survived. Your living and winning make the stories and sacrifices of your ancestors worthwhile. It is in your blood to overcome mountains. Don't assume otherwise.

Your living becomes the link by which the chain is perpetuated and future generations are made possible and viable. Imagine that you are the cornerstone for the future. Upon your back will future successes be told. You set the stage for the next foundation of growth. The mountains that you overcome will inform the mountains that your descendants overcome. The greater the battle you endure, the greater the testimony, the greater the fruit, the greater the hope, the greater the legacy, and the greater the next stage of victory.

Today, I hear people talk about making it big. I hear the chatter about stardom, celebrity, and fame. I hear more talk about the outcome than the process. The mountain speaks to the process. It is not that we should focus on the problem or its enormity; rather, we must acknowledge the merit of the path taken in order to reap the desired outcome. In this instance the mountain becomes the instructor. We learn our mettle. Some mountains bring out our best, previously unknown or unproven. Others highlight our weakness. Still, weakness is not a cause for despair but an opportunity for perfection. Again, perfection is not the absence of error. Rather, it is the achievement of the whole. The testimony of the strong is not that strength is the domain of the few or entitled. To the contrary, strength is within reach of us all, because it is weakness perfected. The mountain perfects you and makes you whole by the lessons you learn and the obstacles you overwhelm. The interesting thing about mountains is that once we scale to the top, the mountain is not destroyed. It remains as a monument to our cause and a respected legacy, and the fame belongs both to the mountain and the trailblazer who conquered it.

In some cases, the infamy goes to the mountain and the glory to the mountaineer. But

Look for Your Mountain

the timid soul gives the mountain too much respect and is stuck in a sense of inevitability. Outweighed by fear, he believes it is certain that the mountain cannot be overcome. The brave heart cages his fear and realizes that the mountain is a crucial opponent on the road more difficult yet more able to reward. The brave heart understands that smart power, not just brute force, is crucial if one step for a man is to become a giant leap for mankind.

Urban Spring

Several years ago, I ran and lost in the local school board election. Though passions ran hot and bitter divisions were drawn, ultimately, the people spoke, and I listened. Still, I fell in love with my city through campaigning. It wasn't the first time that I loved her. Yet I chose her all over again. I relished her complex beauty. Her inconsistencies. Her vigor. Her scent and countenance. Her physique. Her color and hues. Her soul and spirit. Her people. Vying for public office made me a better community servant and taught me the sobering truth about influence. Leaders, in particular elected leaders, deal in the sphere of influence and persuasion. Yet influence can be used for the greater good or peddled for a tactical end. Leaders agitate and collaborate. Leaders vouch and disapprove. Leaders sanction and support or blame and judge. Leaders aren't perfect or absolute in practice or belief, but leaders should be fair, balanced, principled, and forward-thinking. If anything, I've learned what kind of traits I desire in a leader and the brand of leadership I hope to offer: authentic, right-standing, and visionary.

What any servant knows is that you can't lead effectively or compassionately without first serving someone other than self. Leadership is a balancing act among interests and perspectives: between selfish intent and the collective good, between majority rule and minority voice, between private understandings and public admissions.

Urban Spring

Leadership, though at times seemingly arbitrary in the hands of the partial, is that necessary engine for transformative growth. My city lies at a fragile gulf in her history—not a place of weakness but one of delicate opportunity: sink or swim.

As I look upon the world landscape and the revolutions dotting the globe, I know what we need more than ever in our urban centers is not a revolution in arms but a revolution in thought—a radical shift whereby we waylay the status quo and use smart power, strategic power, and smart partnerships and collaborations; where we stop labeling the enemy and start solving the problem; where we are accountable; and where we upend agendas, conspiracies, and practices that seek only to lie to us about our present state or keep us bound in inequity, either self-inflicted or systematically imposed. We need an *Urban Spring*.

I think back to my first experience with Du Bois and *The Souls of Black Folk*. I think back to the passion it ignited—the passion to be excellent and to think critically about intersecting communities and how to build forward with accountability and grace. I reminisce upon a scene I never visited but conjured up in books and imaginations: the Harlem Renaissance. Today's renaissance, like those of yesteryear, would force us out of complacencies and into the vastness of creative and intellectual liberty. Even as a little girl growing up in East Orange, New Jersey, I imagined with near certainty that there had to be something better out there, as if E.T. had phoned home from a forward point in space and time. Though I could not capture the essence of it until now, I understand confidently that we need an Urban Spring.

Our urban centers are the social, physical, and environmental engines for so much of what compels our societies and where our minds and bodies play: culture, art, music, fashion, higher education, corporate industries, and financial hubs. Once manufacturing hubs, too many of our cities, however, have become an afterthought in the wake of economic displacement. Still, where there is a vacancy, there is an opportunity to creatively fill it. If left forgotten and abandoned, our urban areas become a race to the bottom, but when properly invested in; and where abstract and concrete resources are appropriately used; and advocacy, activism, and intellectualism all thrive; then urban centers become the catalysts for widespread and infectious growth. Vibrant cities spill out into suburban spaces, and that vibrancy is exported in the form of merchandise, culture, thought and understanding.

So, when I speak of an *Urban Spring*, I speak of a collaborative stew where we labor to create a forum in action as well as thought, to engage the disparate voices, and to create viable solutions and policies that are not ideologically entrenched. Right now, we are stuck with a scoreboard that categorizes winners and losers instead of flexible

Urban Spring

partners and teams, where the "us versus them" mentality squanders occasions for authentic dialogue and progressive collaboration. An Urban Spring, on the other hand, would afford a nexus where people power, smart power, and creative or innovative power (where the masses demand excellence and expect individual and mutual success) — not pure economic majorities or political powers — rule the day; where solutions are driven by need and aspiration; where opportunity meets diverse and credible expertise, meets community expectation, and ultimately defines value.

In order to go there — to that unexplored mental and physical territory — first we must be willing to challenge ourselves as well as our peers. We must abandon the inferiority/superiority construct and make our goal to create equity and eliminate knowledge disparities. Knowledge disparities help feed economic, health, performance, and aspirational gaps, whereas experience and exposure cultivate new minds and spirits and build destinies foreign to the status quo. In essence, equity is unfettered opportunity: the chance to be heard and the choice to be included. Yes! Second, we must all hold ourselves accountable. Remember, power without accountability is corrupt, advocacy without accountability is paternalistic, and activism without accountability is reckless. But alongside equity and accountability, diversity and dissent must be allowed. Diversity lends itself to collaboration, and collaboration is a different goal than compromise.

Compromise implies winners and losers in varying degrees and shades, and typically the weaker party is overpowered by the stronger. Compromise is not wrong. But instead, collaboration seeks to allow parallel or even contrary thoughts and opinions to coexist where possible, as long as the greater good is served and the various forces are not destructive or wasteful. We must display a sense of honor and integrity in our thoughts, deeds, and standards in both mutual and private space. Honor and integrity breed trust; trust fosters the necessary psychological and intellectual safety for collaboration to occur. Yes! Finally, in that Urban Spring, we must dare to be entrepreneurial in scope, vision, and problem-solving while being rational and practical. Theories can't reside in the abstract and fall apart under real constraints. Rather, when data and best practices are shared and translated into tangible services, policies, and solutions that are able to shuttle across borders and boundaries, then we have applied knowledge, which is powerful.

Ultimately, we must seek to find new ways of value creation and not just better performance according to the commonly accepted rules and standards. Every great movement innovates in a way not previously seen. We need an Urban Spring. If Harriet were here, she would tell us. Martin and Malcolm would scold us like weary parents. Sojourner would demand it of us. Frederick Douglass would tell us that it was indeed possible, and the regal Shirley Chisholm would show us the way. We need an Urban Spring where we uphold compassionate thought and action, and academic and practical expertise; where we collaborate in an authentic manner; where we challenge and revitalize the culture; where we export our excellence, import best practices, and build economies of scope. Yes, we need an Urban Spring!

The Humanist Within: Deconstructing They and Other

Going to high school where I was one of few African American and minority students, I first encountered my otherness. While I stood out for many reasons, being black in an otherwise culturally homogenous environment made me a conversation piece. I often quipped to friends and family that some of the students viewed me as a *black China doll* to be taken down from the shelf, curiously examined, and neatly kept in its proper place. The only problem: I didn't keep my place.

During those transformative teenage years, I learned a lot about myself, including the power of culture to bring together disparate groups; team-building around common, core goals; and how to bridge across barriers. I vividly recall when a friend and fellow teammate called to inform me about race-day attire. During the call she blurted out that this was the first time she had phoned a black person. We laughed. I was not in the least bit offended, because it was spoken from a candid heart. My friend was learning that difference didn't have to be odd, just different. The more meaningful part of our conversation, however, came from her realization that the substance of the call was not unlike other casual conversations between her and white girlfriends. Still, this was a first. It meant that her world was a bit more diverse, and confirmed that we were more than convenient friends who traded polite talk between classes. In that moment she had an epiphany, and it pleased her. At face value she was a white girl from suburbia and I was a black girl from urban America, but we were more than finite categories. Though we had complex peculiarities, we also shared compelling similarities, and more importantly we shared a genuine human connection.

High school afforded many such experiences. While I played the role of other for many who had never been exposed to someone like myself, the lessons went both ways. Though my dad worked in a corporate environment, and we strayed frequently from our city neighborhood, I largely lived a black urban life. Dotted with a few non-black interactions on the other side of the fence, I imagined that white children, and in particular white children of a certain socioeconomic status, had more opportunities. Up close and personal white suburban life was demystified, however. Many of the things I desired (better education, a picturesque home and neighborhood, professional and life success) were not particular to white people, though prevailing stereotypes would have you believe otherwise.

Rather, they were the outcomes and advantages associated with better opportunities and privileges that many whites were afforded. White folks, and even white folks with money, were like black folks in a lot of ways: driven by similar emotions, frailties, inspirations, and aspirations. We were all profoundly human. Were there meaningful and relevant differences? Yes. Were there social inequalities? Yes. Did I fight against them? Yes. Were there prejudices on both sides, which seemingly prevented deep and fruitful dialogue? Yes. Still, I learned firsthand the pitfalls of stereotyping and the generalization trap. I learned that blame only perpetuated inequalities. Denial and forgetting didn't work either. Rather, social accountability and responsible activism should demand people, processes, and practices to change in order to create both understanding and access. I learned that no one individual had the power to make or break my success—not even *the man*.

In high school I learned to deconstruct the terms *they* and *other* and to confront and crawl out of my own boxes while challenging those of my peers. When you remove pejorative labels and invite "others" to dialogue, the "they's" become less sinister, less irregular, and less extraterrestrial, and you realize that one man's *they* is another man's *self*. Too often in a highly fragmented world, we lose sight of our interconnectedness. We lose sight of the humanity in one another. It is when we dehumanize those who are somehow different from us that we excuse ourselves from the bonds that we share. Difference is not a detriment to our society but a gift and a catalyst for innovation, colorful insight, discovery, and greatness. Still, as we honor and respect what makes us unique, we must also honor and respect what makes us alike—

our humanity. As we celebrate our diversity, we must learn to reflect and synergize around what joins us across the vast human diaspora. What has made our interrelationships coarse and disjointed has been the penchant to demonize and criminalize difference and to devalue diversity, whether based on ethnicity, creed, religion, sex, orientation, or the various categorizes of "other."

As long as individuals uphold absolutes and accept the us-versus-them mentality, we give credence to the predefined castes that society dictates. When we challenge our norms and build nontraditional partnerships and alliances; when we're fervent without being intolerant or rigid; when we love and celebrate our differences without denying others their rights; then we begin to appreciate the humanity in one another. Human empathy allows you to consider a human life outside of your own sphere and to recognize the validity of that person's desires, hopes, and thoughts. When you leave room to experience someone outside of your preconceived biases, you invite fascinating discoveries. Rather, when we lose sight of the value of all human life; when we pass over or ignore certain opinions because they aren't our own; when individuals are blurred into impersonal categories or we substitute groupthink for reading the book and not just the cover; then we are our less-progressive selves.

In city politics I've run headfirst into that notion exactly: either you're with us or against us.

Either you support us, or you can't be included, ever. Either you come up the same way I did, or you're somehow less credible. Either you have the right geographic pedigree, or you can't participate. Worse, if you're on a certain team, it's safe to presuppose your positions without the proper queries. As you can see, though I've discussed the context of being *other* largely in an ethnic sense, these issues are not just relevant to black and white. They speak to how we define groups and categorize self versus foreign. For instance, I've had city and community leaders question my blackness, as if ethnicity were a brand—faux versus designer label. Whenever we judge individuals by some vague, monolithic generalization, we fail to recognize the potential innovation and dynamism in our midst. Humans are peculiar and complex. Humans are three-dimensional. And the moment we permit ourselves not to experience the fullness of our kind, we are blinded to the rich possibilities beneath the surface. Difference is not a curse. It is a tool for greatness. Yet understanding human nature is to understand that we are more alike than not. Difference without similarity can be polarizing. Difference with some common chord is refreshing and inspiring. Our hope is in the collective nature of we. Our despair is in our isolation.

Culture as Currency: Building Home Base

As I have written previously, culture is a powerful tool. There is a culture in your home. Culture on your school or job. Culture shared by those of the same ethnic group or color. There is the culture of a nation or geographic region. Even your faith produces a culture, as does your particular church or place of worship. Music and the arts shape culture. Technology does as well. Any interest, passion, ritual, habit, or practice has the potential to build and mold culture. And culture, in turn, has the agency to crystallize thoughts and understanding, whether for the good or bad.

As a physician I've given a lot of thought to that amorphous thing called culture. In particular, I've focused on how to build health consciousness into the popular culture: what I've coined as the "go well" movement or revolution—like going green, but instead, going well. As a community leader, I've labored to build a culture of learning and success, in particular with at-risk groups and underrepresented minorities—always building, always looking to marry stakeholders from one space to another realm in the hopes of crafting some accessible yet bold idea, another brick in the direction of wholeness. Indeed, culture is dynamic, seemingly hard to create in one instance—and in another, almost kinetic and taking form of its own.

Culture has the most impact when it's the currency for some broad-based vision and mandate with mass appeal. For example, culture bookends our political persuasion and voting preferences, our public agenda and policies, and our laws and reforms. Too often, however, we know the divisive nature of culture wars. There are many Americas within one nation. Yet anything that seeks to isolate or trap us into our respective corners is against our progress as a people. Then there are certain understandings (extensions and outgrowths of our culture) that pervade across several categories of self-identification. For example, there is hip hop. Hip hop is and affects music, dance, fashion, language, social awareness, norms, ideals, and even the ballot.

Like there was a hippie America, there is a hip hop America, but more widespread. Hip hop wields influence among different ethnic groups, faiths, languages, geographic regions, and socioeconomic statuses. Hip hop is universal. What started out in the underground as a subculture somehow rose up the ladder and into the cosmopolitan and mainstream, out to middle America, and into corporate space. We now hear news anchors use terms such as "dissed." Even professors speak of "keeping it real," and shout-outs are regular fare. Ghetto somehow became chic and took on a sanitized meaning, nonetheless still stereotypical (e.g., "ghetto fabulous"). Children across the globe *spit* hip hop lyrics, which have become the soundtrack for underdogs everywhere. That is not to say that the culture is without its excesses or problems. It's gone commercial, is mass-produced, and lacks authenticity. It breeds a false glory in crime as a come-up, and paints success as a life with access to women (too often caricatured), fame, money, and drugs. It has morphed from its infancy where self-actualization, protest, pride, and ingenuity were the mainstays.

Still, hip hop in its truest sense has implications far greater than the music dial. Hip hop has certain bravado and panache: to do the unexpected and make you pay attention. Hip hop elected our first black president. Not exclusively, but it was a considerable player. It handed him a built-in audience, and unapologetically won over many converts. President Obama connected with youth, who in many ways represented hip hop America. These kids were socialized differently; they developed a cultural expectation to which an older generation had to warm. These young adults grew up in the culture and relished the idea of a black president; perhaps they thought it was a foregone conclusion. Unwilling to keep their opinions to themselves, these kids petitioned their parents and grandparents to get on board. But as with any culture, once you're in, you must stay relevant, or the culture moves on. I've frequently asked myself, "Chris, are you tapping into the culture that already exists; are you taking chances to drive culture to achieve positive goals? Or better, are you challenging the status quo?" When we don't, it's like walking around with uncashed checks in our pockets—unused power and wasted resources.

The above is only a metaphor. The subtext is far deeper. Culture has undeniable currency, but its actors and observers must be accountable. We must possess a sense of duty and honor to grow attitudes and habits beyond the nascent stage and into a responsible force. In thinking about the broader culture, I often reflect on the culture in our homes and communities. I ask, What are the builders in our midst doing to change and try norms, upend myths, and cultivate a spirit of excellence? Culture has the power to develop insights and perspectives and create a value system. Are we leveraging it to sustain a culture of failure or to spur a culture of social change?

Growing up, it was normal for me to prioritize learning and education, because it was part of my family's honor code: faith, excellence, and hard work. Though neither of my parents held degrees, college was expected of us. Our home was far from perfect, but it was distinctly affirming. Our household affirmed our abilities, nurtured us in a rich, intellectual environment, and exposed us to people and places outside of our four walls and our hood. Though no one in my immediate circle went to a school like Princeton, my home culture made me believe I was worthy of the pursuit. I learned years later that my maternal grandmother served as a live-in caregiver for a Jewish family in a nearby suburb. We had in common Granny, Princeton, and a supportive atmosphere, which dared all to live according to a higher standard.

Culture as Currency: Building Home Base

Bottom line: culture produces certain traditions. And a large part of the traditions that you keep were first introduced to you as a child—if not by your parents or relatives, then by some integral person or presence that sowed into you a sense of doing, being, and becoming. So I take issue with the culture of failure that has crept into our daily living. I take issue with the thought that some problems are too big to solve and too pervasive to dismantle. I take issue with the belief that our children are destined to live out the legacies of their parents, whether good or bad. Too often for children from poor or vulnerable communities, this becomes an excuse for failing to create viable opportunities and right the ship. I take issue with those who quit on themselves, because the barriers and odds against them are harsh. They have been taught to accept failure and to live with unequal and stagnant outcomes. I take issue with institutions, and specifically the institutional inertia that clogs our places of government, business, and education, which are resigned to the mold in ways that are detrimental to progress and stifle change. I take issue with those who prosper yet recognize that our society is not wholly equitable, but do little to cultivate success in another or breed opportunity. I take issue with the selfish mentality that others don't matter.

This is what a culture of failure has produced: a caste system, which solidifies roles according to historical trends. Instead, a culture of progress mandates vision, strategy, assessment, and action. A culture of progress savors the value in disruptive change, and seeks to perfect society for the greater good. The past is not meant to be relived or ignored but to instruct and challenge us forward. Otherwise, we are not growing, and, as a fellow minister once taught, "whatever is not growing is dead."

First and foremost, parents and guardians must do a better job of building home base. From the womb and beyond, parents are the first line of defense. Parental choices are constantly shaping and molding children. Parents define social norms. The home environment is crucial in setting a tone and driving future outcomes. Children are sponges and learn a host of lessons in the home. While no one's home is perfect, some households are affirming, whereas others are complacent and, worse, hostile. In many ways, parents are our most vital cultural architects. Indeed, parenting is an all-consuming responsibility and a complex obligation; parents are needed to instill certain attitudes, beliefs, and practices in their children. Before birthing children, parents should prepare themselves emotionally, intellectually, and spiritually to carry out the task at hand. Parents must commit to learning and leading. Parents must take the oversight and build a home base that is loving, safe, stimulating, mature, open, accountable, and encouraging. A home with such "culture" arms you with the currency and might to take on the challenges that lie ahead. Ultimately, the greatest gift any parent can give is to instill in their child the belief that they can achieve and the motivation to aim higher and excel more broadly.

But what of our children who lack productive home bases? It is imperative that we as a community step up and foster the culture and traditions whereby these children are not confined to the reality of their worlds but hurled forward by bright and honorable expectations. Children spend so much of their formative years in school. Schools must strive to nurture not only excellent student-scholars, but also well-rounded, whole persons. And schools can't do it alone, but schools can show promising leadership in this area. Schools can help build a culture that promotes moral and excellent citizens.

Schools can reinforce critical self-development, and, alongside a network of non-profit, faith-based, and public agencies, can become the arms and legs that our children so desperately need. Schools and learning can't exist in vacuums; they must become the playground for holistic growth. In addition to parents and schools, all cultural stakeholders can and must commit to plugging the leaks and deficits that exist in our homes and neighborhoods. Otherwise, our communities will hang in the balance between those who were affirmed and those who were not. If we don't build *human infrastructure* (a term borrowed from a dear friend and colleague), our communities will be stunted and always under threat.

And the greatest responsibility lies within each heart to summon the strength to be great. As adults we must be accountable for the choices we live and the culture we perpetuate. If each person lived out his greatness, then the world would be a better place. We cannot afford a culture that is passive. We must challenge and be challenged. We don't have to succumb to odds and statistics. We can hear them, but we must question norms as a means to live out a greater future. We can create alternatives. Envision bolder solutions. Culture can serve as that spark, the substance that fills the gaps and voids in attitudes, performance, and outcomes. Culture in essence creates demand and should appeal to the best in human potential. But when it doesn't, souls are malnourished, and our social fabric is undone, our homes are unraveled, and our people go extinct in more ways than one. We can and we must build a stronger home base (i.e., household, neighborhood, community, state, region, nation, and world), and culture can be that currency.

The Economy of Favor

In life I've known many successes but not without failures. I've experienced highs but not without lows. I am grateful for the wins and losses, because they've primed me for greater victory. By grace, I'm walking in favor. There is divine favor. And there is man's favor: when your allies and critics both acknowledge that you matter. I once heard an anointed pastor teach that wherever *favor* appears in scripture, you can insert the word *face*. Then imagine that favor, divine or otherwise, is when you walk in the *face* — the glow — of the person who has acknowledged you. Someone's face is like the power in his or her name or pen. What favor is not is luck. Rather, favor is recognition by others that you possess the necessary stuff to get the job done. Favor is influence. Opportunity. Favor is access and the freedom to create in unhindered space.

How did I gain favor? I did my time. When no one was watching, I committed myself to excellence and the belief that I could be great. I lived and dreamed according to a standard. I loved on purpose. I served without fame. Yet I sowed with expectation. Attaining favor is one thing; however, what you do with favor is something altogether different. Favor in the hands of the few is privilege. Favor in the hands of the reckless is tyranny. Favor in unselfish hands is an instrument for individual and mutual success.

There is an economy in favor. Favor reaps dividends—financial, physical, emotional, political, and in the abstract (such as reputation). Favor creates a platform for impact and leadership by which growth and change can occur. Favor isn't some magic bullet but simply goodwill and the ear of the court. Once you've earned it, it's your time to put up. Either you bring something entirely new to the market, or you improve upon something that already exists. Either you give the consumer something he needs—seen or anticipated—or you give him something he wants. Favor produces an economy where thoughts, innovations, ideas, and products are commodities. When your goods are in demand, your profits grow. The better or more valuable your merchandise, the more prosperous an economy you create. And prosperity is more than money. Prosperity is the ability to create wealth—financial or otherwise—the ability to sustain growth, and the relationships and networks that enable success. When you effect change, prosperity should follow, unless your change rings hollow. Change should yield fruit that otherwise would not have been realized.

Indeed, I want a favor that pays it forward. Today, we live in a get-rich-quick society. It seems that almost anything goes as long as it accumulates wealth. Ill-begotten wealth does little to transform whole communities. Rather, it protects social inequalities. Responsible wealth, on the other hand, challenges the system and aims to level the

The Economy of Favor

playing field. It's the American way to dream big, but in order to dream big, you must first do the things that are necessary. Otherwise, you may kill your dream before it ever takes flight. Likewise, you should live to do something worthy of favor. If not, favor that comes easily, flees easily. Favor that is hard-won possesses a longer shelf life. Like your gift, your fruit, wisdom, charisma, and excellence will make room for you. A person of substance endures. Favor is distinct from celebrity. Find favor, and fame will follow. But fame doesn't necessarily beget favor. Recognize that, and you will alter your destiny and that of communities. Understand that, and you walk as a world-changer.

I lived the bulk of my young life learning and training to become a physician. Despite that honorable endeavor, there was something vital that I neglected. Merit is admirable, but discovery and ingenuity are even greater—value added. Unless your academic pursuits add value for others, your success is merely personal. Now, one could argue that being a doctor adds value to others, and I don't disagree. What I missed is the understanding that alongside treating individual patients, I needed to build something credible for whole communities and populations. That has become my brand of success. Choosing a nontraditional, nonclinical career led me to create ideas, organizations, and prospective businesses from scratch. My greatest influence hasn't come from my professional achievements but from my quest to innovate. A spirit of innovation and entrepreneurship has garnered me the greatest favor and made me stand out from the pack. If I could go back and change anything, I would make innovation a central focus throughout my academic and professional careers.

In our communities we will carry favor by what we build and create. In our schools and homes, we should emphasize the daring and creativity it takes to dream an original dream and then execute it. We need to raise entrepreneurs instead of consumers. Regardless of your brand of talent, ownership allows you creative control and positions you to have more autonomy and impact.

In a society where minority groups still struggle for parity and equity, entrepreneurship, in particular social enterprise, presents an opportunity to fill a void and render social change. There is a certain pride and significance in owning your ideas and thoughts. While we rightly emphasize excellence and outstanding performance, we should likewise prioritize building the future of our dreams. All too often, I encounter bright, energetic young minds that aren't being funneled into constructive opportunities. Unengaged and idle, they wander and stray into mediocrity, apathy, or crime. But if we lavished the greatest favor upon those who choose to change our world—if we choose to uplift, praise, and reward those who commit to such efforts—then we will breed demand. There is an economy in favor. Often I

The Economy of Favor

write and speak about having global perspective as well as local commitment. We must learn to enlarge our tents while working to improve home base. There is a global economy in favor. Global doors will open to those who desire to employ themselves in reputable and standard-bearing work. There are vacancies all about the world, and what is needed are leaders to step up and fill them. When you do, your return is favor! And with favor comes the freedom to build bolder and higher. So dare to dream. Dare to become, and favor will soon follow.

Love Matters (The Matter with Things)

The matter with things is that they can clutter your heart and mind: Things like regret, hurt, and blame. Things like the wrong incentives, unrealized dreams, and blunted passions. Things like a loss of hope, stunted imaginations, or stale joy. Like collecting trophies, you can even get caught up in acquiring positive things, so much so that they lose their significance. Indeed, all things may be relevant, but all things are secondary. Above things, there is love. And love matters: Love of self. Love of family. Love of spouse. Love of friends. Love of purpose. Divine love. Love matters. Sometimes I marvel at how empty our interactions are when they're devoid of love. Love is the engine of life. It's very inspiration. So living without love is plagiarism.

Now, let that thought settle. Are you living an authentic life? I've always been a woman of excellence. It's my mark and mandate. But through the years I've learned that if my excellence lacks love, then my excellence is in vain. I always loved medicine, but it took some time to find the right fit. When I recognized the difference between a profession and a calling, I found true happiness. I found strength in my love, and love carried me out of a clinical career into the diverse roles that I now play. I can boldly say that I love what I do. The greatest wisdom or pearl I can give is to invest in what you love to do. Accept the challenge and name your love, then become it.

Love Matters (The Matter with Things)

People who do what they love live imaginative and charismatic lives. People driven by a source other than love live only a measure of the life they were called to walk. There is sovereignty in love.

In our communities and nation, we need more love, in particular a love that makes us responsible and accountable. People who tear down instead of build up lack love. Oftentimes, building up may come in the form of correction. We need an oath:

BECAUSE I LOVE MYSELF, I STRIVE TO BE EXCELLENT AND SOW THE BEST OF ME. BECAUSE I LOVE MY NATION OR COMMUNITY, I CHALLENGE AND PROTECT IT, DEVELOP AND REFINE IT, AND PROMOTE AND PREPARE IT. BECAUSE I LOVE MY NEIGHBOR, I EMPATHIZE, SHARE OPPORTUNITIES, AND PRESERVE FAIRNESS.

In essence, love informs respect. Love informs expectations and standards. Love is the purest purpose and mandate. Yet everyone doesn't have the same measure of love. Some love with restraint. Others love with doubt. And too few love with openness and honesty. In our ministry, Bishop spends a lot of time teaching on love. He challenges the congregants to check their hearts and judge their love, assessing whether it is true and pure or plastic and trite. Too often we love in the manner we have received love rather than how we should love. My mother showed the deepest love a child can fathom, whereas my father was a more distant man but a dependable provider. My extended family and friends filled in for whatever love I could have lacked. I was blessed to grow in an environment of untainted love. According to my faith, Christ showed the most profound example of love. He became a love sacrifice for all mankind. In history, my ancestors died in the pursuit of justice because of an uncompromising love. So, I owe because of love…

And what do I owe? I owe my love, my excellence, my creativity, my support, my expertise, my fellowship, my assets, my hopes, and my past and my future. So how I live is relevant. Imagine if we all lived because we owed; we might choose to live more reputable lives. Perhaps we wouldn't run from greatness, but we would court it, because we had something to prove. To the contrary, when you believe someone owes you, the more entitled and less ambitious you are. I call that living in reverse or waiting to receive rather than living to do. Instead, when your focus is to sow back into others, you look for opportunities to serve with excellence and love. We need to grow our capacity to love.

Recent attention has been given to the idea of emotional intelligence and its implications for interpersonal relationships. The literature defines emotional intelligence as skill in perceiving, understanding, and managing emotions and feelings. While much of our formal education is geared toward the development of cognitive skills, how often do we emphasize the utility and importance of being emotionally competent? If

Love Matters (The Matter with Things)

we made that investment, the payout would be considerable. Leaders who love spark movements. People who feel loved are fully engaged. Purposeful love brings about change. Whereas ambition is critical for personal success, love is crucial for wholesale progress. It's love that gives meaning to struggle. It's love that preserves you. Love matters.

As with any other thing, your standard of love matters. Aggressive love usurps the rights of others in the exercise of personal gain; however, a love that is assertive strongly advocates for personal desires while advancing the goals of others. In other words, make your love count, and make your love just. Too often we imply that love is divergent from strength. Rather, the strong love freely and the weak pretend that it is irrelevant. The world needs more love. Humans need love: love of self and love for others. When we love our neighbors as ourselves, we create a more cohesive society, more progressive relationships, and interdependent teams. When we cultivate our appetite for love, we become actualized. Indeed, love makes you vulnerable and exposed, but vulnerability indicates delicateness. Being delicate simply means you're valuable and authentic. So give and receive love. Live your love. Challenge your love, and sow in love. The harvest is an undeniable treasure. Love matters.

Peculiar People

Great minds stand out. Too often, those who seek to maintain the status quo rail against those who dare to escape conformity. Fortunately, I've never been one to fit in. In grammar school I stood out physically because I was tall and skinny—a fact that my peers made painfully obvious. Except for those awkward stages, I loved being peculiar. I loved being one of the best students in my class. I loved being a bold public speaker. I loved being "the black girl" who achieved uncommon success. I didn't appreciate the ignorance I sometimes encountered, but I relished being different.

Being peculiar is a badge of honor that I've worn proudly through the years. Peculiarity is my heroic power. I don't possess superhuman strength. I can't walk through walls, stop a bullet with my hand, or spit flame or ice crystals. But I'm an original, and I love it. Unless you're an identical twin, there's no one else with your DNA. Despite that genetic truth, too many settle for being generic copies. Going off the beaten path—whether in your ideas, standards, or practices—can be very rewarding. Being different is one thing, but being different with purpose is the truest distinction. Anyone can choose to disagree simply for nonconformity's sake, but the truly inspired are unique in order to be their authentic selves. Your uniqueness is where your strength is. When you recognize that strength, you begin to build in the direction of your greatness. When you hide or camouflage what makes you particular, you give yourself an excuse to fall short. Instead, we should do away with excuses, and invest in being extraordinary individuals. The decision to be common bears a costly price. Rather, the choice to be exceptional is worth every inch of sacrifice, because the payout is infinite.

No one is born perfect. No one is born complete or even born great. We are made. Indeed we are born with unique potential and the building blocks for a particular future, but each person must decide to cultivate that specialness into an undeniable force for success. What have you decided? Have you listened more to your critics or to those impeccable souls who challenge you forward? Have you agreed with the odds or bypassed them? Have you achieved above your potential, below, or merely as expected? Regardless of whether the expectations are great or small, go beyond those limits, and shock and awe! Each person has a potential or some unique ability; however, too few tap into it or grow it to its maximum state. If we do anything for our children, we should give them the permission to be peculiar and encourage their forward journeys. Discover where your talents are and then make them phenomenal. Your charisma lies in your uniqueness. Your supernatural self is your potential realized—your greatness come to bear.

When I was a child, because of what others perceived to be a masculine name, I was sometimes placed with the boys on the first day of school. Back then I found it to be a curious distinction, but also one that empowered me. My full name is Chris, and, as a woman, that fact alone makes me unusual. My parent's choice of name was prophetic. It foretold of my peculiar nature. It preceded me with a reputation to live out. Would the woman be as original as the name? Not everyone has an uncommon name, but everyone has some remarkable quality hoping to be realized and appreciated. To ignore or cast it aside is a crime, like blood spilled that cannot be put back: A destiny unlived. A dream deferred. An opportunity wasted. When we live to be normal or assimilate with our peers, we become some monolithic tribe afraid of our own individuality. We live as we are told. The unexpected remains unexplored space. Out there, waiting to be discovered, are our greater selves. If we give up now, there is a future that will never be. Yes, time will go on, but it will be unmistakably different. Each life has something to add. If no two snowflakes are the same, then why do we limit our trajectories by being followers of an unimaginative kind?

I pledge to live out loud. To be heard. To sing that peculiar song in the key of Chris! It might not sound like your symphony or fit your taste, but it will surely add to the human complement and bring to the earth nectar that the universe needs. Each person has a role to play—a lane in

Peculiar People

this race. And for each role there is an audience that watches and waits. Tap into your audience. How can they hear you unless you dare! There is something to be gained through your unique brand of excellence. Indeed, there is room in the rainbow. If anyone tells you otherwise, they're unsatisfied with the shade of grey they have chosen. When life tempts you to be average, find the courage to be different and unusually great. Because that is what the world needs. One man's greatness does not preclude another's. Rather, it enriches the whole. So pledge to be the "you" that the world needs—uniquely great, uniquely different, uniquely bold, and yes, uniquely you!

Exodus: Looking for My Land of Milk and Honey

In the biblical book of Exodus, we find the story of Moshe, who led the children of Yisrael out of Egypt, their place of bondage, and in pursuit of Canaan, their land of promise. Yet Egypt had not always been a place of adversity. Rather, the Israelites first found refuge there from famine before suffering slavery at the hands of Pharaoh. Then came deliverance in dramatic, miraculous fashion. In exodus they sojourned in the wilderness for forty years. Yet they lacked no provision. Still, many died there, except for two faithful servants and those who remained equipped in heart, mind, and spirit. According to the text, multitudes died because of their disobedience. Even so, *Exodus* was very much about the road to redemption and path chosen for their purpose.

Having said that, I pose the question: How many of us are faced with a similar fate? Living *shackled* by hardship or despair and perhaps low expectations, we crave a way out; however, when opportunity unfolds unexpectedly or too slowly, we fashion a graven image as a substitute for what we think we're missing. Instead, what is the price of enduring and finding those hoped-for pastures? What is the real cost? At some point everyone needs to "go west" to reach that land of promise—not as a fishing expedition, but because their growth and survival depend on it. To fulfill what *is* for you, you must be willing to leave what is not. In

Exodus: Looking for My Land of Milk and Honey

many ways, exodus is a departure from conformity and the status quo. It's a metaphor for getting out of the way of your wildest growth and into your destiny. To know your fullest potential, you have to be challenged in a course uncommon to your routine and environment. You must step outside of perceived norms and go with true inspiration. But true inspiration comes from a source greater than you or one who is informed in some unique perspective.

Being inspired means that you've been sent by some overwhelming and consuming truth. To the contrary, if you harbor fear, regret, or hurt, you'll be less likely to strike out into the vast expanse. Still, what is the promised land? What of milk and honey? It's leaving nowhere in order to get somewhere. It's leaving mediocrity in order to find the ingredients to your masterpiece. It's seeking peculiar greatness in spite of the limitations in your backyard. Exodus is a means to a spectacular end—one that forces the world to take notice.

Frankly, if you've never left your proverbial home, never voyaged beyond the convenience of familiar thoughts and understanding, if you've only lived and died in the same space, what can you really profit another? Perhaps you do not have the means to travel; however, ideas aren't bound by the same fences that bodies are. And hearts and imaginations can elope to destinations real or abstract. In essence, each person needs to leave the safety of concrete opinions and expectations and be bettered by experiences found only on redemption's road.

Exodus is a composite of two Greek words: *ex*, meaning out, out from, out of, or away from; and *hodos*, being a journey, highway, or means. Initially, I was drawn to the word and topic during a recent sermon ministered by Bishop. The message was entitled "Ex'odus," in which he emphasized the redemptive nature of leaving one place for another ordained place, all as a stepwise process in your journey. The text that Sunday spoke to me in deliberate and purposeful ways. Each man is called to walk his exodus as a way to be purchased back from his transgressions and those afflicted upon him by others. Yet, "some are vying to stay in the same place, position, and circumstance that they've been saved from — saved out from," were the words that resonated the most. I put the same question to you that he put to us: Are you seeking home in the very place that you've been delivered from? If so, why? Why do we so often choose the comfort of familiar things at the expense of forward progress and realized prosperity? It boils down to trust. Do you trust that your past has been better to you than your future will be? Or do you believe wholeheartedly that the prospects of the future portend in your favor? Do you believe in a capable future?

On exodus it is imperative to believe in the power of your future. Otherwise, you risk growing restless and distracted along the journey or perhaps hostile to the emotional, physical, or spiritual

Exodus: Looking for My Land of Milk and Honey

demands of your pursuit. The more successful souls understand that pursuit is perpetual and isn't merely acquiring one finite outcome but the process of the journey itself—the thrill of the promise and finding purpose in each successive stage of your life. It is less about an awareness of self and more about knowing that you are called redeemed, forward, whole, and greater than the fallibility that is common to us all. Again, leaving Egypt is akin to leaving a place that once was refuge but became hardship when it no longer served to promote your end. Egypt is whatever does not add value to purpose, and exodus is your mission out and into the next phase—your promised way. But it all starts with leaving! How many Egypts have you clung to when you should have abandoned them? Ask yourself, is it time to go?

You need exes in your life: stages you've been called out of in order to discover the richness of what lies ahead. It's called development. But when you pine for the past, you become like the biblical character Lot's wife. She looked back when she was commanded to flee, and she turned to a pillar of salt. When we fail to embrace our progress, we disintegrate and waste away instead of feeding our forward potential. We get in trouble when we remain in something from which we've been freed already. And those who trust more in their pasts likely fear their futures. Yet the future belongs to her who can see and hear forward. It belongs to him who remains hopeful in his promise. But if you make your home in the very place you've been delivered from, you will not see change in your life nor will you provoke change in the life of another. Therefore, exodus doesn't have only personal consequences but also has consequences for generations and communities alike. You were called to exodus first for yourself, then for another.

Sometimes the path to exodus is a two-lane corridor. You may be drafted to pull someone out, even if that someone is you! Like Harriet, you may need to take several trips back into Egypt to deliver greater multitudes than had you escaped alone or remained tucked away in your freedom. While some things must utterly die in the wasteland, other things are worth being reborn on the other side. Ultimately, exodus is the path to realize what can be if you feed your promise and give it room to breathe.

When was the last time you sought such room—room to explore, unfurl your wings, and soar above the richest earth? Exodus isn't about leaving responsibility but about being accountable to your greatest future. It's not abandonment but the chance to redeem and harvest your calling. It's finding purpose, which is precisely when promise and potential are fulfilled. As long as you stay *caged*, moving forward will appear contrary to who and what you are and may become. However, if you break free—in exodus—and remain steadfast in your purpose, the earth will not be able to contain the depth of your treasure.

Poems

A righteous melody can be made from the
shortcomings of our past encounters.
— Dr. Chris

Letters to My People

To the
Broad-nosed and thin-lipped, wooly-haired and
Bone-straight
(My people);
To the
Freckle-faced and blue-eyed, wide-hipped and
Tie-dyed
(My people);
To my vanilla bean and midnight blues,
Shades of red, brown, and yellow too,
A palette of creeds and creatures with similar and
Dissimilar features
(My people):

Born of His inspiration, one blood coursing across
Man's dispensations
From generation to generations — to the souls of
Humanity;
This is your call to greatness.

Here and now, in this open place — organic and
Dynamic
Thoughts crash and collide in theoretical space;
Despite strife and discord, out come healing and
Grace.

At times we rightly disagree
And raging hearts flare up and compete.
But widened gaps become adhered lines, from
Miles apart to hands intertwined.

The many and few, betrothed in victory, each soul
Must choose—
People, we can't afford to lose.

We must lead together and not be timid! Run this
Race decidedly to win it.

Whether radical or conservative,
(Unimportant, the spectrum of persuasions)
Problems know not affiliations.
Yet they call to your greatness.

We can be different but not hopelessly divided,
United but still compellingly defined,
Set aside, but coalesced for goals of truth and
Progress.

My people,
There are degrees of knowing and hues of perspective—
But the spoils belong to the hearers of this missive.

Not in My Bloodline

It's not in my bloodline to fail.
It is not within me to quit.

I am greater than the phoenix.
Indeed, this is no myth.
I come by way of struggle.
Resilience is deeply etched within.
I am warrior, who suffers long.
Courage is a faithful friend.
I am hope indestructible.
It is in my very bones.
I am that balm in Gilead.
Together, we shall be atoned.

I stand on broad and sturdy shoulders,
Run with mighty winds at my back.
I come. I see. I conquer.
It's not relevant what I lack.

My past is there to teach me;
My present, engaged and by my side.
My future, steadfast, awaits me;
My history, others cannot hide.

It's not in my bloodline to fail.
It is not within me to quit.

We live because of those who did not die.
It is our duty to exist.
Forget not your sacred people.

Already, they overcome.
You owe them more than respect or pride.
Mediocrity must be undone!

Rebel, and walk in freedom.
Flee the tyranny of your sin
Less fear, doubt, and ignorance
Deceive and do you in.
Rebel, and walk in freedom.
Flee the tyranny of your sin
Before the stench of despair
Does tempt you to give in.

Believe not the lies of circumstance,
Which betray your inner strength.
With certainty wear your promise.
By virtue you shall win.
If ever you grow weary,
Regroup and start again.
Time is not your enemy
But a witness to the end.

It is not in your bloodline to fail
It is not within you to quit.

Spit and Mud

Great miracles happen by simple means.
Rare possibilities surface when you dare dream.
Unexpected vessels, paired with uncommon hope,
Solve many problems, despite magnitude or scope.

Whether clay, dirt, green earth, or pearl beaches,
Hear and comprehend what the parable duly teaches.
Surely, the miracle lies in faith that is expedient —
Yes, compelling faith is that critical ingredient.

Imagine that blind man healed by the Light:
Up from the pool, he rose with new sight.
Imagine his first taste of vision and that righteous disquiet
The swell in his spirit, which it did elicit.

Sounds of joy groaned from the belly deep
Uttered for the value of what he did reap.
Though it started with substances indeed not rare,
His gain buoyed him to the height of new air.

Spit and mud, brick and mortar, pen and pad
By faith, erecting monuments in places once wasted;
By faith, arousing expectations in minds before barren;
By faith, sparking aspirations in hearts once foreign.

Worry not when destiny delivers you the impossible.
Do not surrender when all seems improbable,
For what can render a garden from one mere bud?
None other than faith, which empowered spit and mud.

Hip Hop America

Hip Hop:
A lesson in discounted expectations.
Who knew this art would indelibly rock a nation?
Pioneered in more than music and beat,
Rap became a culture that galvanized the street.
It started
An infectious rhythm that told a conscientious story
About more than inner-city dreams or ghetto glory:
Up-front critic of social disparities,
Authentic storyteller about harsh realities,
A different world where kids on the block
Were mythic creatures
With poetic skills and heroic features.
It spread
Not only black art but art for all people.

This ode is about more than music; it's about
The power of culture and how we should use it.
Hip hop Americans, loyal to hip hop swag,
Raise hip hop flags;
In boardrooms and schoolrooms,
Rich folks represent *ghetto fab*.
The irony:
Colors of the rainbow all bop to the same hook;
Hip Hop's gone academic in scholarly books
Revolutionizing generations and communications,
What we wear, what we think—
But is the real Hip Hop going extinct?
This ode is about more than music:
It sings the power of culture and how we should

Use it,
Not abuse it and mass-produce it, but induce
A consciousness and relevance
That reimagines a different intelligence —
An awakening that breaks down barriers, not a carrier
That imports and exports stereotypes and caricatures.

Hip hop.
This ode is not just about the music
But the power of culture and how we should use it.
Who knew the block's underdog would infiltrate Americana?
As trendy as Hollywood, as thorough as the hood,
Wherefore art thou gone — what's good?
How you charmed a nation
From your classic days of righteous indignation
To popular phenomenon and unaccountable celebration.
Hip hop America please stand up, grow up,
Show up and out;
Play your position, be the engine of social invention.
You're still untapped; I want you back.

Hip hop!
This ode is about more than music:
I sing the power of culture and how we should use it.

If I Could Put This City on My Back

If I could put this city on my back,
I'd bear it like lashes on Christ;
I'd wear it like his Passion in the Garden of Gethsemane,
Bruised and ultimately denied thrice.

If I could put this city on my back,
I'd book-bag it and take it into the finest
Institutions of learning;
I'd tool hood scholars into book scholars
And book scholars into neighbors;
I'd bulldoze crack houses, reform jailhouses,
Free poor houses, purify church houses,
Rescue lost houses, raid corrupt houses,
Erect true houses, and win white houses.
Together, we'd stick up ignorance and belligerence;
On the corner we'd shackle excuses, heal all abuses,
And see that hood scholar become that book scholar
And that book scholar become that neighbor!

If I could put this city on my back,
I'd revolutionize revolutionists, update the rhetoric,
Teach all to appreciate Yah's humanity,
And celebrate the diaspora of ethnic diversity.
I'd turn drug dealers into green tech entrepreneurs,
Picture them as wise professors, make gangbangers
Into heroes of the operating room theater,
Not committing bodies to dust and stealing breath
But snatching back lives from the claws of death.
If I could put this city on my back,
I'd bow down and take the burden.

My cross in tow too heavy to bear, together we'd drag it
Screaming to that finish line called grace.
I believe all people have a stake in this race!

So, brick by brick by brick
I'd lay it, soul by soul by soul
I'd pray it, seed by seed by seed
I'd sow it, weed by weed by weed
I'd pull it, child by child by child
I'd raise it, school by school by school
I'd teach it, dream by dream by dream
I'd tell it, hill by hill by hill
I'd climb it, valley by valley by valley
I'd walk it, truth by truth by truth
I'd preach it, love by love by love
I'd live it, drop by drop by drop
I'd bleed it, tear by tear by tear
I'd cry it!

I'd do it, I'd do it, I'd (really) do it:
I would be your Esther if you would be my Mordecai
And together, we would put this city on our back—
Yes, I will put this city on my back.

Go Down, Moshe

When you stand before your Pharaoh,
Know that you've been sent.
Armed with mission and purpose;
Otherwise, he won't relent.
He may laugh and rile against you,
Harden too his boisterous heart—
Still, stand with expectation,
Unequivocal from the start.

When you stand before that Pharaoh,
How you stand is truly key.
If you go with speculation,
He and others may mock in glee;
But if you stand with truth and power,
Unashamed of whom you are,
That fox will surely tumble
And regret you've even sparred.

When Pharaohs huff and puff
And try to blow your house down,
Do not scurry away defeated;
Arise, and defend your crown!
You've been chosen among the called
And predestined from the womb.
If history is a teacher,
Pharaoh will learn from his tomb.

So, go down, Moshe,
Way down to Egypt land.
Speak before that stubborn Pharaoh;

Make known your right demands.
Go down, servant Moshe;
Stand firm before his throne.
By the end of your commission,
Your legacy will ever be etched in stone.

Road Map to Greatness

"Don't die without ever having lived great."
These are the words carved into my heart,
That echo through my soul,
And linger in my mind's fragrance.
A spiritual yoke, they call to me,
Compelling me ever so near,
Pushing me forward and along the way.
My yellow brick road—that road map to greatness.

Greatness is found in the life you impart.
It happens rarely in an instance
But comes from an authentic knowing
Your call, your purpose, your mandate.
Not the stuff of fairytales or even childhood dreams
But the meat and matter of your mark:
Your soul's yearning, your spirit's cry;
Where aspiration mates inspiration And births destiny
Along that yellow brick road—
That road map to greatness.

Whether red lights, stop signs, detours
An occasional U-turn,
Or through the briar patch,
May you find your road.
Atop a soaring mountain,
Or a lonely stretch of street—
In an epiphany's flash,
May you find your road.
In the day you find it, the earth will applaud
Her people will resound.

For greatness breeds value that others need,
Fulfills necessities,
Shapes the desires of hearts,
Meets vacancies seen and unseen,
And seeks to endow and train.
If not, you might behold success but never be truly great—
Like the difference between living and breathing:
Intimately alike but figuratively miles apart.

"Don't die without ever having lived great."
Walk that yellow brick road—your road map to greatness.

Water Will Find a Way

Like water I'll find a way
To break through rocks and dams,
And overrun levees and roads.
With tenacity and heart, I'll find a way

To beat back obstacles and barriers,
Nagging odds, and bitter forecasts.
I'll press on and remain.
Like water, I'll find a way:
I'll surge, I'll meander, I'll babble, I'll ripple.
High tide, low tide, rip tide, or eerie calm,

Like water I'll find a way.
Dismay, disapproval, and denial won't silence me.
I'll rise up like a surfer's wave.
Brute force or quiet strength,
Like water I'll find a way.

I'll go where the river leads,
No matter how far or wide;
Border cozy shores and deep-sea floors;
Go boldly into the unchartered;
And carve out new territory.
Like water, I'll find a way.

Under pressure, I won't crack,
But I'll find a way.
I'll scold the desert
And soothe the forest,
Choose my state and form as needed:

White glaciers, blue waters, brown lakes,
Hot geysers, warm oceans, or frigid bays.
Like water, I'll find a way.

No one will be able to contain me
Or tame me.
Like water, I'll find a way.
No season will defeat me.
Like water, I'll find a way.
No condition will outperform me.
Like water, I'll find a way.
No location will stymie me.
Like water, I'll find a way,
Whether hidden in a cactus or an oasis in trouble.
Like water, I'll find a way,
Whether plenty like the seven seas
Or few like a narrow stream.
Like water, I'll find a way,
Whether raging like a storm or still like a pond.
Like water, I'll find a way.

I'll quell the fires and replenish the earth,
Even flood the land with my prowess.
I'll stay as long as I'm needed
And recess when my work is done.
Like water, I'll find a way.
I will endure through the ages
And greet descendants across time,
Give energy to the dead and neutral,
Birth life in known and undiscovered places.
Like water, I'll find a way.
Like water, I'll find a way.

It's Morning

Alas, it's morning time,
And each morning brings revolution on the day,
Rebelling against darkness,
The sun peels back the night sky,
Overcoming an opulent moon,
Heralding that good news:
An awakening!
Redemption. Retribution.
Resurrection. Reconciliation.
It's morning time,
And each morning brings revolution on the day.

Never monotonous,
Each dawn commands attention:
New horizons granted.
New destinies understood.
New radiance and audacity.
New thought. New hope.
New drive. New glory.
Bright inspiration. Bold rebuke.
Yes, it's morning time,
And each morning brings revolution on the day.

Overpowering,
The sun glows with insight and revelation:
Unfettered truth
An obvious mandate,
Never recycled light
But fresh illumination,
A mantle passed on into future—

A promise.
Tell me, is it yet morning in your thinking?
Has wisdom dawned?
Morning, in your living and doing;
Morning in your belief;
Morning in your struggles and dreams;
Sunrise in your passion, a second coming in your faith.
I pray it's morning time
Because each morning brings revolution on the day!

For the Love of Words

For the love of words,
I write this.
For the love of words,
I breathe this.
For the love of words,
I fight this.
For the love of words,
I do this.
For the love of words,
I become this; I manifest this.

For the love of words—
Not he said or she said,
But for the love of words:
Those spoken into the atmosphere;
Words that break silence;
Speak power; crush fear.
For the love of words:
Words that amass movements;
Words that take formation;
Speak dominion; undo confusion.
For the love of words:
Words like vows, oaths, and decrees;
For the love of what He spoke;
For the love of things that matter
And have been written before me.

Words
Words that ignite justice
Words

Words that spark understanding
Words
Words that provoke revolution
Words
Words that consummate passions
Words
Words that voice freedom
Words
Words that march and protest
Words that soothe indignation
Words that hold accountable
Words that challenge and champion

Words
Words that encourage and teach
Words that crawl out of boxes
Words that love and forgive
Words that unify and coalesce

For the love of words
Words that bear burdens and satisfy costs
Words that negotiate peace
Words that predict and foretell
Words that reform and cultivate

For the love of words
Words that speak victory
Words that listen and hear
Words that walk the globe
Words that speak plainly yet profoundly
For the love of words
For the love of the Word in me

Reflections and Affirmations

Success is not the fruit of circumstance
but the offspring of deliberate intention.
—Dr. Chris

Even liberty has laws.

Excellent minds do inspired work.

Don't allow struggle or frustration to alter your destiny. Instead, scramble for the victory.

Excellence is without honor
in the home of mediocrity.

A made man is one of conviction.

Never prostitute your soul for a quick win. Rather, endure faithfully and labor for principled success.

Get inspiration off the bench.

Let cowardice die and audacity prevail.

Live life colored outside the lines.

Belief is a door. Doubt is a prison.

Poverty of the mind is a yoke.
What you think you can't achieve, you won't.

Decency is the fruit of dignity — the capacity to be ever human yet imitate the divine.

Leadership may be situational,
but it should never be convenient.

Uniqueness is the key to confidence.
Yet too few find it.

Love is the single greatest factor and the most searched-for unknown.

Your greatest legacy lies in your ability to create your most meaningful difference.

Tears don't make you weak.
They make you human.

Debate is good for the soul
if you think before you speak.

Being a bold, independent thinker
is foundational to greatness.
It is the ability to inform imaginations.

A man who never dreams
is a broken and hobbled soul.

From life no one is exempt.

Love should be felt more than it is spoken.

Speak to love, and it will speak back. But speak love, and you will reap love's harvest.

While your capacity to give love is your greatest gift to bestow, your ability to receive love is your greatest reward to self.

Love is not the acceptance of all things
but the ability to treat all souls with
compassion and dignity.

Love should hold you accountable.

Who and what we love, along with how we love,
is the truest reflection of our souls.

A weak heart fails to love.
A brave heart longs to forgive.

You must fire mediocrity if you plan to prosper
and divorce complacency if you hope to thrive.

Prettiness fades. Smartness endures.
But a beautiful soul is forever.

True beauty grows with time.

Even excellence is an art.

Harvest life like you would a garden.

Don't despise shortcomings. Empower them.
Don't trust in shortcuts.
Create unconventional solutions.

Goals are achievable when you view them as a
process instead of a finite outcome.

To be poor in spirit
dims expectation and invites despair.

Don't allow people, places, or things to define
your character. Rather, allow your heart.

Knowing your purpose is akin to knowing your
name. It is utterly necessary.

Not knowing your purpose is like asking a
stranger to tell you for which cause you were born.

Hate is incompatible with life.

A free man owns his thoughts. A caged man
thinks only what others give him the comfort and
permission to believe.

Thinking is free, but its value is in how
often, how well, and about what that will
determine your worth.

Don't look for a dividend if you
didn't make the investment.

Endangered minds think too little. Extinct minds
invite others to think for them.

Though we are born human, we can live as heroes
and choose to die divine.

The merit of a man is in the
significance of his choices.

Even in your low point, have dignity and faith.

I art life.

Distractions cause you to neglect your purpose.
Devoid of purpose, you lack clarity, and without
clarity you succumb to what is.

The difference between being good and being
great is in the significance of the details.

Don't give someone else the power to
write your story when it is you who will be
judged by the events.

Life should not be lived according to the
odds against you. Otherwise, will and
individuality are irrelevant.

The measure of life is in the affirmative.

Amount matters when it comes to faith. A lack
of faith will count you out. A little faith will save
you, but great faith will change the world.

Go where faith leads.

The creative soul lives on through his creations.

Creative minds build the dreams that others hope to be real.

Do more, and you will become more.

Love does.

A fearful man never really lives, and a bold man doesn't die.

It's not the presence of fear that limits you, but the power you give to fear that casts the deciding vote.

Creativity applies to more than art. Creative thinkers and builders help solve our way out of boxes.

Rethink what is art, and you'll live a better, bolder, and more imaginative life.

Forgive your way out of a dark past.

Forgive more, and you'll reap grace.

Forgiveness doesn't excuse accountability. Instead, it liberates a captive heart and spurs your growth.

A smile encourages your soul.

Imagine if we laughed more together.

Community is not measured by
physical space but by the heart.

Empathy is better than tolerance.
And love, more powerful than respect.

Go well. Be whole. Live happy.

Being a world-changer is
more than a slogan but a mandate.

What you make a priority testifies for or against you. Who you commit to, answers how you feel about yourself.

Apply what you learn to the greatest good.
Otherwise, you will be ripe with potential
but have little impact.

Information represents knowledge to the learner but creates understanding when we share it.

What you give up matters when
what you gain is of no consequence.

Know the difference between repentance and surrender. To surrender means you are out of options. Rather, repentance represents contrition and the hope to do differently.

A great man outlives his wrongs, outlasts his
adversities, and overruns his fears.

You can't have generic faith if you
desire a specific outcome.

Being contrite is the beginning of a thing.
Producing new fruit is the fullness thereof.

Lies should always offend your sensibilities, but
hearing truth should cause you to grow.

Never take a lie to heart, but
embrace truth in your bosom.

Zeal is a powerful force in the right hands and a
dangerous weapon in the soul of the bitter.

There is never a good reason for apathy.

Be free at last but not the last to be free.

Never forget the people who honored you when
you could not honor yourself. Honor those people
all the days of your life.

Open your tool chest.

Be radical for excellence.

Excellence belongs to whoever chooses it.

There are many rungs on the ladder of change.

Excellence should not bicker with lack but go boldly and do.

The Pledge

I pledge to be the "me" that the world needs: uniquely great, uniquely different, uniquely bold, and yes, uniquely me.

About the Author

Dr. Chris T. Pernell, a dynamic physician-leader and health and wellness visionary, has strived to heal and transform souls. In her public health practice, she concentrates on community-based health promotion and advocacy and worksite wellness programs, emphasizing a holistic approach to total well-being. Specializing in vulnerable populations, she has sought-after expertise in health and wellness consultancy and prevention strategies.

A cum laude graduate of Princeton University, she attained her medical degree at the Duke University School of Medicine and an executive master of public health in healthcare management from the Columbia Mailman School of Public Health. Dr. Pernell trained clinically before segueing from medicine to population-based care. Recently, she began the Johns Hopkins Bloomberg School of Public Health General Preventive Medicine Program, where she helps facilitate local, regional, and national public health and preventive medicine projects.

Dr. Chris, as she is affectionately known, founded My Body & Me as a faith-based initiative to combat overweight and obesity and associated chronic illnesses. My Body & Me has expanded to include diverse audiences, spearheading the use of novel prevention practices for engaged, healthful living. In particular, the program was adapted for the public school setting with workshops for parents of school-aged children, and as a series for the residents of the Essex County Juvenile Detention Center in Newark, New Jersey.

Dr. Pernell was selected as a contributing writer for "Health Care Rx," an online expert panel conducted by the *Washington Post*, where she submitted weekly blogs on the health-care reform debate. AOL highlighted one of her pieces as the best of the web in their weekly series. In *Letters to My People*, she affirms the unique greatness of each person and hopes to empower others to tap into their highest calling and abundance. Through creative genius, faith, and profession, she vows to make world-changers out of the sea of humanity.

Dr. Chris serves as an ordained minister in the fivefold leadership of Bet HaShem YHWH Worldwide Ministries, Inc. From North Carolina to South Africa, she has actively combined her passion for faith with her vision to improve the health and well-being of individuals and communities. Alongside her mission to heal, she labors as Director of Bet HaSHEM (the Praise & Worship Ensemble) and founder of YAHSpeak, an inspirational spoken-word performance group. Raised in East Orange, New Jersey, she has made Newark her home and purposes *to raise* her city to the standard of global beacon and urban gem. In these efforts she ran for the local school board and vows to use the pulpit of public service to agitate for social change and justice.

In the words of Dr. Chris, she has made "the pursuit of cultivating whole, well, and equipped souls" her life's work and enduring legacy.

Made in United States
North Haven, CT
05 April 2023